TRAINING FOR COMPETITION

JUDO

COACHING, STRATEGY
AND THE
SCIENCE
FOR
SUCCESS

Hayward Nishioka

"It is not the critic who counts, not the man who points out how the strong man stumbles, or where the doer of deeds could have done them better. The credit belongs to the man who is actually in the arena, whose face is marred by dust and sweat and blood; who strives valiantly; who errs, and comes short again and again, because there is not effort without error and shortcoming; but who does actually strive to do the deeds; who knows the great enthusiasms, the great devotions; who spends himself in a worthy cause; who at the best knows in the end the triumph of high achievement, and who at the worst, if he fails, at least fails while daring greatly so that his place shall never be with those cold and timid souls who know neither victory nor defeat. "*

—Theodore Roosevelt, 26th President of the United States and a brown belt judoka

TRAINING FOR COMPETITION
JUDO
COACHING, STRATEGY AND THE SCIENCE FOR SUCCESS

Hayward Nishioka

Black Belt Books, Valencia CA 91355
Copyright © 2010 Cruz Bay Publishing, Inc
First Printing 2010
All Rights Reserved
Printed in South Korea

Library of Congress Number: 2010934976
ISBN-10: 0-89750-194-2
ISBN-13: 978-0-89750-194-1

Edited by Sarah Dzida and Wendy Levine
Cover and graphic design by John Bodine
Photography by Thomas Sanders
Cover photos by Eric Nishioka and Gary Goltz

For information about permission to reproduce selections from this book,
write Black Belt Books, 24900 Anza Dr. Unit E Valencia, CA. 91355

For information about bulk/wholesale purchases, please contact 1 (800) 423-2874 ext. 1633

BLACK BELT BOOKS
A Division of **OHARA** PUBLICATIONS, INC.
World Leader in Martial Arts Publications

TABLE OF CONTENTS

Dedication..6

Foreword 7

Chapter 1:
To Coach or Not to Coach? 10

Chapter 2:
Mapping Out a Strategy to Win 16

Chapter 3:
Advanced Judo Tactics...30

Chapter 4:
A Family of Techniques..52

Chapter 5:
Scouting Your Opponents 72

Chapter 6:
Communicating With the Competitor 82

Chapter 7:
Cardiovascular Conditioning 90

Chapter 8:
Resistance Training...102

Chapter 9:
Nutrition and Weight Management 130

Chapter 10:
Dealing With Injury..142

Chapter 11:
Risk Management...156

List of References by Chapter 160

About the Author 165

DEDICATION

This book is dedicated to the memory of a great American judo leader: Frank P. Fullerton.

FOREWORD

The traditions in judo remain much the same by virtue of history and basic principles. However, each generation does define the style of participation, and coaches are held to responsibly analyze and adapt to the current trends of this living entity.

The core commitment of professional coaching is to bring out an individual athlete's personal excellence through physical conditioning, strategic planning and developing skill. Coaches mentor their athletes toward success and to develop their own competitive insight in order to exceed their expectations. Coaches also endeavor to predict the actions of opponents. Therefore, coaches use their personal education and experience to ask the right questions about each athlete's unique case and guide him or her to excellence.

Each coach has a method of training a judo athlete, but I believe Hayward Nishioka has captured the comprehensive guide of what is necessary to be a winner in the sport of judo in this inspired manual. There are many vibrant and illustrative photographs of junior *judoka*, but don't be fooled into thinking this book is for developing young competitors alone because it is not. Chapters about cardio-vascular and resistance training, nutrition and dealing with injuries are scientifically well-founded and applicable to judoka on all levels. While some areas in the book—tactics, strategy, scouting and, to some degree, legal issues—may change over time, it is more important to see the spirit of adaptation that is uniquely demonstrated in these chapters. Hopefully, readers will glean or emulate something that may improve their own brand of judo. If this is done, perhaps we will each be able to make a personal contribution to improving our judo coaches, athletes and nation.

—Dr. Jacob Flores
2010

"Man cannot discover new oceans unless he has the courage to lose sight of the shore."

—Andre Gide, Nobel Prize winner, French novelist

To Coach
or Not to Coach?

CHAPTER ONE

To Coach or Not to Coach?

bviously, a competitor is interested in enhancing his performance. Who does he look to do this? In judo, like many other sports, the competitor probably looks to a coach.

A coach is an essential partner to an athlete embarking on the competition circuit. Coaches should not only be mindful of short-term goals like winning championships but also of how to shape the character of future citizens, which is especially true for child athletes. Coaches act as vehicles of transformation. They help the athlete move from one place, physically and mentally, to another.

"Coach" is a magical word. A coach is the person you want to be able to go to for information. A coach is your friend, brother, sister and mentor all rolled into one. If you happen to be the coach to an athlete, you need to have answers, or at least a way to help the athlete get them. And sometimes, you just need to know what the athlete needs. It could be something as simple as moral support during a match or shouting directions. Or it could be something more like helping the athlete learn what went wrong during a competition and how to correct it. Coaches give athletes insight. Coaches help competitors learn to be champions. If you're looking for a coach, you're looking for someone to anticipate or answer athletic needs.

So how do you go about finding a good coach? Do you need one? What are the qualities that an athlete has to look for in a coach? Once found, what are the athlete's responsibilities to himself and his coach? What should coaches be doing to help their athletes? How much is your time worth? These are some questions to think about as we begin our journey.

Queries

1. **What does a coach do?**

2. **Who needs a coach?**

3. **What does it mean to "fill your glasses full?"**

4. **What kinds of sacrifices do champions make?**

5. **What sacrifices do coaches make for their athletes?**

What to Expect From a Coach

In most instances, students grow up practicing judo in a *dojo*. If the dojo is a reputable one, it will have a number of people in it who have taken a judo coaching certification course from one of the major judo organizations. These are usually minimal courses that ensure several important things:

- that the coach is a member of one of the major national judo organizations.
- that these members, who are in key leadership roles, have had the proper background check and screening.
- that prospective coaches have had some introduction to the intricacies of coaching.

If you are a competitor in a dojo, you may be assigned to one of these coaches.

Coaches should be knowledgeable not only in regards to technical judo but also as to how the body works and how to get it to its maximum potential. Coaches should be aware of the rules of the tournament. They should understand advanced judo tactics. They should be willing to go the extra mile, like scouting, to get athletes to the performance level they need to be for competition. At the same time, there is another quality that a coach should have that is difficult to quantify. And that quality is more intuitive—does the coach have a heart? Is he caring of his or her athletes and not just looking to find a body to do his bidding and extend his ego? Does he care about individuals? The art? The science of judo?

This coaching manual should be of use to the coach and competitor. For coaches, it will provide them with a road map of dimensions to get their competitor to the top. For competitors, this manual will offer insight into the many facets a coach should help bring to their training preparation for competition. Of

Photos by Pamela Yamane, Kaizen Concepts

One of the most important roles that a coach takes on is being there for his or her competitor's greatest moments of triumph and of insecurity.

course there are some competitors who will be able to "coach" themselves, but training for competition is a multilayered process and it helps to have the deft guidance of an effective coach.

What to Expect From the Competitor/Coach Relationship

Doctors recommend that adults drink eight glasses of water per day for optimal bodily function. What would happen if you only drank four glasses every day? You would probably be able to function, but you wouldn't be working at your highest capacity. You are only drinking half of what you actually need. The lack of liquids could cause a pH-balance shift in the body, and this deficiency could cause more stress in your kidneys and nervous system.

Think of judo competition in a similar way. How full are your glasses? How complete is your cardiovascular ability? Or strength? What about your glass of techniques? Are you just taking a few sips or are you drinking fully from the cup by the end of the day? What about strategy, tactics, nutrition, etiquette and knowledge of the competition rules? Which glasses do you need to fill so you can function at your best on competition day?

The competitor/coach relationship should focus on this idea. The coach is present to help the athlete balance his or her daily intake of these "liquids." The coach looks at the glasses and tries to help the athlete balance the liquid in each. If the competitor is deficient in his or her cardiovascular glass or needs to put more liquid into the family of techniques glass, then the coach should be able to note that and help the competitor fill up.

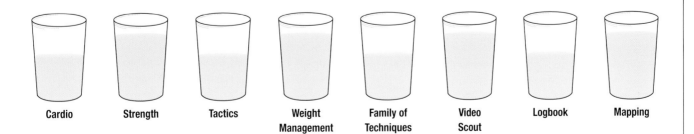

| Cardio | Strength | Tactics | Weight Management | Family of Techniques | Video Scout | Logbook | Mapping |

There are many different kinds of competitors. For example, there are competitors who are young children, and there are competitors who are adults who just want to be involved in a fun activity. These competitors don't really want to compete seriously, but because their dojo has a monthly tournament, they participate in a match or two. Then there are recreational competitors who find the challenge of competition stimulating; they tend to enter regional competitions. This person wins a few matches and loses a few, but he or she eventually earns enough points to be awarded a black belt. Then there are the serious competitors. They find judo to be magical and they tend to win more than lose. This kind of competitor practices more than the usual twice-a-week and does auxiliary training like weightlifting and running. Beyond the serious competitors are the professional *judoka* who compete at the national and international levels. The sensitive coach will always be aware of the competitors' capabilities and tailor their preparation and competition goals with those in mind. The coach should be aware of the kind of competitor he or she has and should know how to address the goals and "glasses" of that individual competitor.

There are also many different kinds of coaches. There are novice coaches who are well-intentioned and generally just encourage their competitors from the sidelines. There are recreational coaches who have coaching experience and can spot some inadequacies in a competitor's "glasses." These types of coaches probably can point out these deficiencies and help the athlete train to correct them. In fact, some of these coaches can be very good at this. Professional coaches are the kinds of coaches who understand the game and know how to prepare their competitor before a tournament. They know how to advise the competing judoka and they know how to help the competitor improve his or her game long after the match is over. The better coaches, no matter their level of experience, will always strive to continue their education in coaching. They expand their knowledge base not just on techniques but on kinesiology, biomechanics, exercise physiology, sports psychology, weight training, refereeing, nutrition, etc. For the coach, it is a never-ending process of self-betterment as well as improving the athlete. Of course, each coach will differ in his or her philosophies but all should be interested in bettering their students.

Competitors are in need of a coach if they are looking for help. In turn, a coach should be looking for an athlete who is looking for guidance, who is interested in being the best and who is driven to get there.

Of course, the competitor/coach relationship can succeed in unexpected and different ways. Take the example of a 13-year-old Hispanic player at a tournament in Southern California. The youngster was new to judo competition. He had lost his first match in under 10 seconds. He was determined not to be bested in his second match, which, if he lost, would eliminate him from the tournament. Like a street fighter, the youth pushed and pulled wildly. In his desperation, he missed openings and pushed himself to exhaustion after three minutes of nonstop flailing. The youth lost by a *wazari* to his opponent.

The boy bowed off the mat, fighting strong emotions and tears, and was met by a man in a tie who pulled him into a hug.

"Boy! You did great," the man said cheerfully. The man was Gibbs Dibrell, the boy's coach.

Later, another coach approached Dibrell. He asked Dibrell how he could say that to his competitor. After all, the boy lost.

"Yeah, he lost the match," Dibrell replied, "Maybe I didn't train him well enough. But he's a champion in my book. That boy comes from a low-income, single-parent family in a tough neighborhood.

He's never done anything like this organized sport. He was heading toward joining a gang, but he joined us instead. He borrowed a *judogi*. I had to do a lot of fast-talking to convince him to come today. It took a lot for him to get out there and put his ego on the line. When I go back to the dojo, we'll talk about all the things he felt and what he gained today in his test of courage. Next tournament, we'll do better."

How Much Is Training for Competition Worth?

The competitor needs to think about how much he or she is willing to sacrifice to get to their individual goals. The higher the goals, the more sacrifice the judoka will probably have to make. A talented athlete working out twice a week may win a local event, but it's a different story if that same athlete wants to go to a national event with only 100 workout sessions, no auxiliary training and no coach.

Of course, athletes sometimes form major goals while traveling down the judo highway of life. He or she may think: I've come this far so maybe I can go further. Whatever the goals may be, the question is: What are you willing to sacrifice in order to get there?

For the coach, it is important to know how much the athlete is willing to sacrifice in order to achieve his or her goal. Why? The coach has to know whether he is coaching a weekend warrior or a committed athlete. The more committed the judoka, the more time a coach will have to devote to his athlete. For the coach, it is an investment of time and effort that the coach doesn't want to waste on an uncommitted athlete. He could just as easily devote his time to a committed athlete as to an uncommitted one and yield higher dividends. A coach only has so much time to give.

In a sense, the relationship is an implied contract for the competitor and coach to help each other. That way, after the training, preparation and all the sweating before a competition are done, both the coach and the competitor can feel proud in the work they've done to get there.

Perceived Value

The U.S. Olympic Committee estimates that it costs close to $1,000,000 to produce an Olympic gold medalist. Coaching is an integral part of developing a competitor who can perform at the highest levels so it is not uncommon to find some coaches charging $50 to $100 an hour. These, however, are some of the best coaches in the country. Lower-level coaches may charge $10/hr. while still others with very little experience will sit in the coach's chair and yell at referees for free.

Generally, an individual coach's prior competitive records and ability to produce champions determine prices. However, coaches must consider how much their time is worth.

True/False

1. Coaching is about more than just winning a championship.

2. A good coach is a vital portion of the equation for success in high-level judo competition.

3. Knowing what condition an athlete is in is vital to developing a plan to improve on deficient areas.

4. The "glasses of water" metaphor illustrates areas that need to be worked on by judo athletes in order to succeed.

5. Compensation for coaching is non-existent.

Answers: 1.t, 2.t, 3.t, 4.t, 5.f

Chapter Review

1. Discuss the relationship between coaches and competitors.
2. Explain the importance of a good coach and what he or she should know minimally.
3. Discuss what types of activities better coaches participate in.
4. List the areas of improvement needed in order to compete in high-level competition.
5. Briefly discuss coaching compensation.

"We need to know where we are going and how we plan to get there. Our dreams and aspirations must be translated into real and tangible goals with priorities and a time frame. All of this should be in writing, so that it can be reviewed, updated and revised as necessary."

—Merlin Olsen, NFL tackle, sportscaster and actor

Mapping Out a Strategy to Win

CHAPTER TWO

Mapping Out a Strategy to Win

You turn on the television. Lo and behold, the National Judo Championships are being televised. You can't believe your eyes as you quickly phone your judo buddies. The color commentator, Jimmy Pedro, gives some historical background on judo Olympic medalist Ronda Rousey—her age, height, weight, background, strengths and weaknesses. Pedro discusses what the audience should expect, how hard she has trained this past year in preparation, what players will possibly give her trouble, and what she may do to overcome those problems. You probably switch on your TiVo because you want to know this information. What if you're coaching a competitor who may one day get a chance to fight her? What if Rousey's in the same division as you? No matter whether you're a coach or a competitor, you should be asking: What do I need to do to have a real chance at winning?

2008 Olympic silver medalist Ronda Rousey is a successful *judoka*. How did she get there? Have you mapped out a strategy to be as successful as her? What things do you need to consider?

Queries

1. **What's the difference between strategy and tactics?**

2. **What does it mean to map out a strategy?**

3. **What are timelines and markers?**

4. **Why is time awareness important?**

5. **What is so important about knowing your environment, self-assessment, scouting the opposition and devising a long-term plan of preparation?**

6. **What is meant by "setting markers" and recording your progress?**

7. **Why is assessing, reassessing and adjusting your progress important?**

Strategy vs. Tactics

Strategies are long-term overall plans to overcome restrictions to success, whereas tactics are methods of dealing with more immediate problems. The former is more aggressive while the latter is defensive in nature.

Tactics actually are only a part of your strategic planning. In strategic planning, it is usually decided what has to be accomplished in order to be successful. In a sense, your strategic plan is a road map to your objective. Often the items that need to be accomplished in your road map are listed in a specific order. You need to get to first base before proceeding to second base, third and, finally, home plate.

Following a prioritized order that gradually prepares one for the next step, then the next, is called grooming. Grooming is practiced so that a person feels a sense of accomplishment and progress. The trick is not to choose a task that may be too difficult and result in failure and, over time, disillusionment. There should be a sense of progression. You want to accomplish achievable tasks first and then build on them.

These incremental time slots in which you train for progress are referred to as a timeline or training period. The overall process of going through these training periods is called "periodization."

Periodization depends on the activity and the specific goals you are trying to achieve. Your training periods can be as short as a week or as long as a quarter of a year or more. Mitchell Palacio, an exercise physiologist at City College of San Francisco who trains elite judo athletes, suggests a three-week period after which he finds diminishing returns for the efforts expended. By this, he means that your gains in strength, technique or physical ability tend to plateau. For example, let's say you can bench-press 200 pounds but you want to bench-press 300 pounds. The first week, you bench-press 225 pounds easily. The second week, you go to 245 pounds with a little more work. By the third week, it's getting harder to get to your goal, and you've only gotten to 265 pounds. These are diminishing returns. So the question is: Would you rather spend the extra weeks getting to your goal or on other areas of concern?

Of course, if you had more than three weeks to train, your timetable would allow you to bench-press 300 pounds or whatever else is your goal. So the thing to remember is that periodization depends on your individual needs and the time you have to accomplish your goals.

This type of thinking is different from recreational judo in which students attend practice just for the fun of throwing around a few bodies and chatting with friends before going home till next practice. There is nothing wrong with this type of judo, and it is enjoyable and good for your health. Nonetheless, if you're hoping to become a champion and your time is limited, you can't afford to work in a judo void. Think about it this way: If even elite athletes, who have been training since they were 15 years of age, only get to enjoy the prospect of being part of four Olympic Games, then you have got to have direction. You've got to have a strategy.

Timelines

Timelines are important because they delineate sections of time in which certain goals are to be accomplished. Remember the "glasses of water" example in the last chapter? There are many dimensions to a competition, and you need to make sure that your "glasses" for aerobic and anaerobic conditioning, strength training, technical ability, tactical understanding, etc., are full; those are your goals pre-competition. Timelines will help you get your goals accomplished. These goals, once accomplished, are referred to as markers.

So let's say that you are coaching an athlete who has just attended his first national championship but only to watch. He has been in judo for a couple of years now and wants to compete in an event … maybe next year. As the competitor's coach, you should be thinking about the following: What are his vulnerabilities? Is your athlete physically strong enough? How about his physiological condition? Can he last through five minutes of fast-paced competition? Will he know what to do if the opponent wants to drill him into the mat far enough to find a new route to China? Does he have the technical ability to throw, pin, choke or execute an armbar on a high-level competitor? The answers to these questions will help you set the competitor's markers, which will in turn become the things he needs to accomplish before becoming championship material.

The Judo Athlete Inventory

There are skills you need to succeed that you are probably not aware of. That's where a good coach can come in handy. What about finances? What about getting some experience before competing at a high level? After you have your markers, how should you start?

A good place to start would be to take an inventory of areas that need to be improved on to be competitive. You should take inventory from time to time to see what progress you've made. Here is a chart that will help you organize your progress. The chart includes only a suggested list of important areas, but it can be changed to suit your needs.

	Goal	Present	Done Today	Comments and Recommendations
Cardiovascular				
Strength				
Neck				
Shoulders				
Chest/Back				
Abdominals				
Hips/Legs/Calves				
Standing Techniques				
Front/Back				
Left/Right				
Circular				
Touch and Go				
Combinations				
1.				
2.				
Counters				
1.				
2.				
Gripping				
Transitions				
1.				
2.				
Ground Techniques				
1. Pins				
2. Chokes				
3. Armbars				
Tactics				
1.				
2.				
3.				
4.				
Psych. Preparation				
Additional Comments:				

Think of this chart as an inventory that you or your coach does every one or two weeks to see the change in progress. It's a good idea to keep them all so you can note areas that need improvement.

Logging It

When you're in the midst of training and making every effort to succeed, it's easy to lose track of your progress. Whether you're a coach or a competitor, log your practice. All you need is a simple logbook, a writing instrument and time to write down your observations. These observations will act to quantify your current progress and leave a historical record for what worked and what didn't. You may have your own items of importance but here are a few suggestions you might want to include in your logbook:

You can write your observations down by yourself, with your coach or in a group. No matter how you do it, logs help you solidify future plans. For example, you can write something like, "I was thrown two times at the weekend competition, but I threw my opponent three times. Next time, I'll shoot for more throws and not be thrown at all."

Date:

Place:

Goals (aerobic, anaerobic, strength, technical, tactics, video breakdowns, rules, etc.):

Opponents and your practice against them:

Interesting observations:

How you felt about your practice or learning event:

Recommendations:

Below is an example of what a judo student might write in a daily logbook. Note that the student includes goals that address tactics, rules and his weaknesses because he lost to a left-handed competitor in a prior competition. His log is as follows:

True/False

1. **Strategies and tactics are the same thing.**

2. **Periodization is a process devised to optimize performance within a given time frame.**

3. **In considering timelines and markers, you should see where you stand by entering a major tournament.**

4. **These are examples of markers: building a family of techniques, being able to sustain seven to ten rounds of nonstop *randori*, lifting 200 pounds over your head in quick succession at least five times, etc.**

5. **It's impossible to keep track of your progress during training.**

Answers: 1.f, 2.t, 3.f, 4.t, 5.f

Date: March 28, Saturday

Place: Seinan Dojo

Goals (aerobic, anaerobic, strength, technical, tactics, video breakdowns, rules, etc.): I need to get used to practicing against left-handed opponents. My goal for today: Get three good ippons off the grip against three fairly good left-handed training partners.

Opponents and your practice against them: I was able to accomplish only two ippons off the grip because there were only two-left handed partners available.

Interesting observations: I found it hard to get in on left-handers because the stance was different. The grip was also very different. Although I was able to get into the throw on two of the opponents, the throw still felt awkward.

How you felt about your practice or learning event: I felt fairly uncomfortable because I'm not used to adjusting my hands to the stance. But I felt like I learned a lot.

Recommendations: I need to continue practicing against left-handed opponents. I'll also review the videotapes that my coach made during practice.

One-Year Strategic Map: Long-Term Strategy

Let's say that you plan to compete in a national championship next year. This means that by competition time, you should be in top physical condition, in the cardiovascular and muscular areas. You also need to build on your techniques by possibly adding two or three new ones. Don't forget that you need to know the rules as well as how to train to use the rules to your advantage. You should also test yourself in smaller tournaments to see what progress you are making.

All of these markers have to be achieved in the time frame of one year. That's 52 weeks or maybe 50 weeks, depending on if you take a vacation somewhere along the line. So, 50 weeks times two practices a week is 100 workouts. If your workout is an hour and a half but your actual randori practice time lasts about an hour, then that's only 100 hours to hone new skills. If, like most recreational players, you rest every five minutes, your actual *randori* time, in which you get to work under stress conditions, is about 30 minutes. For most recreational players, that's only 50 hours of serious practice time a year. Is that really good enough? If you are a really serious player, you need to be working out four to five times a week. That would give you more than 100 hours of randori time.

The following lists will outline general two-, four-, six-, eight- and ten-month strategies to consider when taking a year to prepare for a competition.

First Two-Month Period: Things to Do

1. *Ancillary training:* Jog 20 minutes at your target heart rate on alternating days with weight training.
2. *Evening training:* This should include randori practice. A portion of the training sessions should be devoted to learning a new technique to add to your family of techniques.
3. *Log it:* Arrange for someone to videotape your workout sessions as well as your tournament matches. Study and record practice and tournament outcomes, such as who threw whom how many times, with what techniques, and in what time span. Apply the same effort with mat work. How much time do you rest in between workouts? What was the quality of your sparring partners? From these assessments, you should formulate some recommendations as to what needs improvement.
4. *Other:* Should a local tournament be available near the end of this two-month period, compete. This is optional, and if you do it, don't expect to see that much of a difference after training hard for just two months.
5. *Notes for coaches:* You should keep a logbook because that becomes your baseline. From this baseline, you can now determine what progress your athletes are making over time. Are they stronger, faster and in better shape? Are they throwing more people with a wider array of techniques in different directions? Can they last longer without needing a long rest between workouts? What things do they need to work on? Additionally, your athletes should maintain their own logbooks. Instruct them on what should be recorded. From time to time, you can compare notes and see what your athlete is thinking.
6. *Markers:*
    a. Attain and sustain an aerobic targeted heart rate of 220 or the maximum equivalent that your THR should be, depending on your age, work output and whether you are exercising for a minimum of 20 minutes. The equation is 220 – Your Age x 0.7. (To learn more about your THR, see page 93.)
    b. Increase your resistance levels by a minimum of 20 percent.
    c. Increase your family of techniques by one technique.
    d. Increase your ability to study your judo. Assess where you are and what needs to be improved on.
    e. Maintain a logbook.

Second Two-Month Period: Things To Do

1. *Ancillary training:* You should continue running and aerobic training on alternating days with weightlifting but with an increase of 10 minutes to 30 minutes at your assigned THR. Add another

10 percent increase in the resistance training area. In other words, do more work over a longer period of time.

2. *Evening training/logging it:* Continue randori sessions. From your previous video study sessions, some recommendations should have been forthcoming. During your randori practice, you should make a concerted effort to deal with some of those recommendations. Whatever the problem is that you should have written down in your log, it should be practiced until corrected. Do not forget to add a new technique into your athlete's family of techniques. Also, do not forget to log your entries and continue to make assessments and recommendations.

3. *Other:* In addition to the video reviews, a stellar judoka will study the tournament's rules and use them to his or her advantage. He or she will also be aware of uniform requirements. (For more on how a uniform can impact your success in a tournament, see Chapter 3 page 39.)

Know the rules, especially as they pertain to the *judogi*. Here, a judge measures the length of a competitor's *gi*.

4. *Notes for coaches:* If there is a local tournament, enter your athletes in it. (If you are the athlete, you should compete.) If it is near the end of the fourth month, you should begin to see some differences, especially in the strength and cardiovascular areas. If your athletes are in better shape, they should be able to attack more times per minute without fatiguing. The more attacks they execute, the better their chances of throwing and winning in judo.

5. *Markers:*

   a. Increase your strength factor by a minimum of 10 percent.

   b. Increase your endurance factor by a minimum of 10 percent.

   c. Add another technique to your family.

   d. Get the right equipment and the right practice partners.

   e. Your log entries should reflect an increase in your proficiency in throwing. This means that you are not only attempting more throws but are completing them in practice and in tournaments. Keep an accurate count of these. The upward or downward count may be used as an indicator of progression or regression.

   f. Don't forget to always reevaluate your recommendations.

Third Two-Month Period: Things to Do

1. *Ancillary/Evening Training:* Whatever you or your athlete's needs are, you should now be thinking of trying to approach the anaerobic threshold—the amount of work you can do in a given amount of time—during your morning and evening sessions. You can do this by increasing your target heart rate. Instead of multiplying by 0.7, go to 0.75 or 0.8 for a minimum of 30 minutes. That's 220 for men or 225 for women minus their age multiplied by 0.75 or 0.8, which will equal the target heart rate at which your athletes should be training for a minimum of 30 minutes. From your videotapes, you should be able to determine certain areas of your or your athlete's body that may need strengthening. Begin to increase resistance in those areas. For example, if your training partners are easily freeing themselves from your grip, you need to increase your gripping strength.

As you are working on specific areas, try to apply plyometric principals into your exercises, especially in *tachi waza* or throwing techniques. (For more of these kinds of exercises, see Chapter 8.)

2. *Logging it:* Review videotapes of practice sessions and tournaments to determine where you've improved or where you need to suggest improvements. Write out a plan of corrective measures to shore up deficiencies. Write out the results of your efforts in your logbook and, of course, make further recommendations. Remember that recommendations may come from assistant coaches, partners or yourself. Recommendations encompass many aspects and may include working on different elements of your judo, such as gripping, quicker attacks, developing a left-sided attack, countermoves, your use of mat space, physical conditioning, strength, tactics or groundwork. Whatever the area of need, you want to concentrate on it for the next two months.

3. *Other:* If a local tournament is available, enter it with a plan of attack that includes the techniques and skills that you have been practicing over the last five or six months. Although there is a tendency to fall back on old techniques, developmental tournaments should be used to see what, if any, progress has been made. It's not about winning at this juncture; it's about developing a wider range of options.

4. *Notes for coaches:* In reviewing your recommendations, you may find that your athlete does not have a combination move or countering abilities. For example, maybe your athlete is very good at attacking from the right side but now her training partners are used to that strategy. A couple of combination moves that address a right and left offense could be the new addition to her family of techniques. It's always a good idea to have techniques that work in combination from multiple directions, i.e. front and back or left- then right-sided attacks. It could be that your athlete's first attack is a fake right move that causes the opponent to lean in the opposite direction and overcompensate. This allows the athlete to use her second attack, which is a throw in the opposite direction. Or it could be that the first technique truly failed, and the athlete's second technique is actually a back-up technique to clean up the mess.

5. *Markers:*
   a. Your athlete should be in fairly good physical condition by six months. His or her THR should be 75 to 80 percent.
   b. You should be able to sustain a randori workout of eight five-minute rounds with eight successful throws. This means that you are practicing against eight different opponents for five minutes each for 40 minutes total.
   c. Your evening workouts should reflect more workouts with less rest time in between and a greater variety of techniques. As coach, you should be pressing your suggestions.
   d. You have learned and are able to execute several techniques in combination.
   e. Your win/loss record should be improving and should be recorded in your log. If you are coaching an athlete, you and your athlete should record this in your logs.
   f. Your ability and confidence to execute techniques should also be reflected in your log entries by the higher number of successes.

Fourth Two-Month Period: Things to Do

1. *Ancillary training:* Continue to monitor areas that need extra resistance training. Also increase weight, intensity of exercise or both, and duration of conventional or plyometric exercise as needed.

Now we are going to kick it up a notch in our physical conditioning routine. Your conditioning should be groomed enough to add bouts of interval training and *fartlek* training. (For more on fartlek training, see Chapter 7 page 95.)

2. ***Evening training:*** For six months, you have gradually increased your body's ability to withstand the stress of a sustained and elite training schedule. You should be able to go through an hour workout session with five to six high-level sparring partners with little to no rest between practice sessions. You should be able to execute a technique at least every 30 seconds with appreciable success. Because you're learning to attack at a higher rate, your opponent must defend more, and this taxes his energy stores. If he wears down physically, he will wear down psychologically as well. Because you will hopefully be in better physical shape than your opponent, your opponent will begin to make mistakes you can take advantage of. These successes should also build your confidence.

3. ***Logging it:*** Out of your collection of videotapes, select one or two of the opponents with whom you always seem to match up at local tournaments. Next, fill out a competitor profile sheet. (See Appendix A for the competitor profile sheet.) As many tapes and matches as you can find, fill out a profile for each. These should include not only your matches but those of other competitors as well. After reviewing them, make your recommendations and implement them into your practice sessions.

4. ***Other:*** If there are no pressing recommendations from your previous two-month period, add low-risk attacks to your repertoire. Low-risk attacks are attacks that can be done with little risk of placing you in a disadvantageous position or the opponent countering you. These techniques may include, but should not be limited to, *ippon seoinage*, *kouchi* to *kuchiki daoshi*, and *soto makikomi* and fading to the outside.

Photo by Pamela Yamane, Kaizen Concepts

These techniques are easily done from a one-handed position or from a non-contact distance. The main purpose for these types of techniques is to throw the opponent but also to act as an easy remedy to the 25- to 30-second rule. This is a tournament rule that states that a substantive attack must be made within 25 to 30 seconds or else the competitor will receive

Here, a competitor executes a low-risk attack near the boundary line. Because the opponent resists, the competitor avoids the noncombativity penalty.

a penalty for noncombativity. (Should you have the opportunity to implement your plan during a tournament, be mindful of the preparations you have made. From the results, you'll see if you need further corrections, and these should be noted in your log.)

5. ***Notes for coaches:*** If your judoka is on track and free of injuries, you are most likely finding it tougher to find him or her good workout partners. That may be because your athlete is improving exponentially beyond the recreational bounds of judo, and his or her dojo partners just can't keep up anymore. As the coach, you may need to turn down the volume of the athlete's sparring.

Teach your judoka to "play fight" like lions and bears wherein the stronger animal allows the weaker animal to have the position of dominance. This way your athlete keeps the less skilled sparring partner interested in practicing with him or her; it's for each partner's mutual welfare and benefit. You can also "dojo hop" with your athlete. It is always interesting for both parties because the fight for supremacy is with an unknown entity in an otherwise normal setting.

In recent years, the importance of mat work or groundwork has become essential to your competitive game because of the advent of Brazilian *jiu-jitsu*. Anyone aspiring to be a champion cannot afford to neglect this skill set.

6. *Markers:*
   a. Increase cardiovascular sustainability under adverse conditions.
   b. Be able to avoid noncombativity penalties by executing a low-risk attack.
   c. Be able to fill out a plan of attack by the use of the competitor profile form.

Fifth Two-Month Period: Things to Do

1. *Ancillary training:* Maintain your anaerobic threshold level. Studies done at The USJF/City College of San Francisco's High Performance Judo Institute lean toward an approximate 180 THR for young athletes of 18 to 25 years of age. For elite athletes, it is important to maintain excellence in this physiological domain because many athletes subconsciously feel less of a need to rely on their aerobic/anaerobic conditioning as their technical skills improve. Basically, they think if they can beat an opponent in a minute, then why train to last the extra minutes?

2. *Evening training:* If you haven't done so by now, you should start to practice transitions with your sparring partners. Transitions are moves that transition you and your opponent from a standing position to ground position, like a pin, choke or armbar. These are not chance moves that just happen. Instead, they should be practiced moves that are a response to the opponent losing his balance and falling into a specified position. The best time to apply these moves is when the opponent is reaching the ground or has just hit the mat. Usually, these transition maneuvers have a higher possibility of success if they occur within two or three seconds.

3. *Logging it:* From your video analyses, devise a plan of attack by listing the techniques you plan to employ on specific opponents and sparring partners. See how accurate your plan is when you spar/compete with them. If your initial strategy doesn't work, then your plan should be subject to change. Don't forget to write down the results of your encounter so you can make further recommendations. If you should see a particular weakness for which your competitors may not have a responding technique, then you should consider that gap in their game. One thing you might note while watching your videotape is your physical actions. Sometimes, an athletes tries so hard that he has an instinctive reaction that causes his body to engage the opponent before his mind does. This usually happens when the athlete has been working hard and is hungry for success. You should be aware of such occurrences and put them in your logbook.

4. *Other:* By this time, you should have developed a family of techniques that allow you to attack in any direction, counter or do combination moves, attack off the grip, and execute a low-risk attack—that is, if you have been diligent in your planning and execution. Your physical condition

should also be excellent and enable you to handle all the eventual stresses of competition. However, remember that in competition, as in life, nothing is a sure thing. If you are a wise strategist, you will continually try to prepare for the unexpected. You don't want to be surprised by changed tournament conditions. You want to prepare for all eventualities. In other words, be adaptable and not rigidly set into one mode of thinking.

5. **Notes for coaches:** Tournament play is the testing ground for your athlete. If you haven't been doing it already, it is the time to test out what you have been practicing with him or her. Before you sign up for any tournament, make sure you know what type of tournament it is and how your athlete is going to fight it. Is it a winner stay-up tournament, a single or double elimination or a *repechage* system? Is it a developmental tournament or a real-tough championship tournament? Is your goal to try something you have been working on with your athlete? Or is it that you just want him or her to win?

6. **Markers:**
   a. Maintain a high degree of physical conditioning.
   b. Be able to make quick transitions.
   c. Be able to plan for adaptability and change.
   d. Understand different tournament models.

Final Two-Month Period: Things to Do

1. **Ancillary/Evening training:** The final two-month period is when you want to start tapering. This is a concept used in many high-intensity sports and involves gradually lowering the intensity of your workouts, perhaps a week or two prior to your targeted event. Often, athletes are so wound up near tournament time that this is when injuries tend to occur. During the last two weeks, you may reduce your randori sessions and replace them with technique drills you want to improve on instead. Or you could use this time to improve on your mat skills. What you are trying to do with tapering is give your body time to heal and rejuvenate for the upcoming event. You're also minimizing your chances of being injured just before a competition. Many judo competitors think they have to work out every day before the big event. Some also believe that their skill level will diminish without a last-minute practice. However, resting and scaling back your training far outweigh these minor losses. Wouldn't you rather feel well-rested instead of fatigued and sore on competition day anyway? In the end, the wise competitor fills in the missing randori sessions with more *uchikomi* and *nagekomi* or mat work practice sessions. A couple of days before the target date, the competitor may not engage in any physical activity, save for a few uchikomi drills, if any.

2. **Logging it:** One year of preparation should find you ready for the big event. Look at your logbook and compare what you are now to what you were one year ago. It should fill you with confidence.

3. **Other:** Split this final two-month period into separate months. Determine how intense you want your workouts to be during those last two months. During the first month, review all that you've been working on. In the final month, start tapering in the last two weeks. Generally working at about 75 to 80 percent of maximum THR capability with periodic bouts of 90 percent to 100 percent is advised. This can be within the individual workout session where you work at 75 percent the entire session, or intersperse your 75-percent rate of intensity with 90-percent rate of intensity, perhaps for tougher randori partners.

4. *Notes for coaches:* Your athlete's physical condition should be excellent by now. The randori practice should reflect an ability to get good grips to execute a diverse family of throws. On the ground, the judoka should know how to pin, choke and execute an armbar, as well as other defenses. Your student's knowledge of the tournament rules is to a point where he or she can understand how to avoid penalties or force the opponent into making errors. You've also helped your student learn how to modify the practice intensity level to where the athlete can blow away the opponent or toy with the opponent for awhile.

5. *Markers:*

   a. Reduce chances for potential injury with tapering.

   b. Increase THR to 90 percent.

   c. Continue improving strength and technical proficiency.

   d. Win the tournament.

Chapter Review

1. Discuss the difference between strategy and tactics.

2. List at least five markers in progressive succession you want to achieve.

3. Discuss why periodization, markers and logbooks are important.

4. On a sheet of paper, devise a logbook entry for one day of practice.

5. If you are a coach, think about whether your athlete has only one favorite technique. List what marker you would set for your athlete for a three-week periodization.

True/False

1. In mapping and periodization of a one-year program, your goals are best accomplished in two-month increments.

2. The early portion of the periodization is an assessment period in which you find out what you need to work on.

3. By the fourth period, you should be at maximum cardiovascular conditioning.

4. Tapering occurs about a month before your main event in order to avoid injury.

Answers: 1.t, 2.t, 3.f, 4.t

"Too many people are thinking of security instead of opportunity. They seem more afraid of life than death."

—James F. Byrnes, U.S. Supreme Court Justice

Advanced Judo Tactics

CHAPTER THREE
Advanced Judo Tactics

Let's say Julio is an athletic competitor from the Dominican Republic. He readies himself for a competition by purchasing a brand new single-weave judogi at the tournament because he is thinking only of convenience; it is lightweight, cheap and good for travel. At the tournament, his first opponent is from Great Britain. The British opponent steps on the mat wearing a heavy double-weave *gi* that is barely legal and hard to grip.

On mat "B" of the same competition with about two minutes to go, the American judoka Karla is behind by a wazari that resulted from receiving three penalties—two for noncombativity and the other for intentionally stepping out. Now she has her back to the line again, but if she steps out one more time, she'll lose.

In another match, her fellow teammate Sam is ahead by a *yuko* early in the match. The coach is yelling at him to remain on the offensive because he wants Sam to maintain the lead. Sam complies, but by the final minute of the round, he fades, gets thrown and is caught for a wazari.

What did these three judoka have in common other than the fact that they all probably lost their matches? The answer is, none of them were aware of how to use advanced judo tactics.

"Advanced judo tactics" means working within the rules and environment of a judo competition and gives you a distinct advantage in your matches. If you know how to tactically navigate rules, environment and time in a competition, it will help you emerge as the winner, which is the goal of a champion.

Queries

1. What does history have to do with the nature of judo rules?

2. How do *judoka* score?

3. Are there penalties in judo competitions?

4. Are there special tactics you can use in judo competition?

Historical Basis of the Rules of Judo

Judo is a derivative of *jujutsu*, which is a traditional Japanese martial art originally created for killing or maiming an enemy. For the jujutsu practitioners of long ago, the only rule was to win by any means necessary. However, in the 19th century, Japan underwent a period of modernization known as the Meiji Restoration; it was an era during which Japan discarded feudalism in favor of the modern world, trading traditional swords for modern guns. This era also helped lay the groundwork for judo founder Jigoro Kano to change the face of the Japanese combative martial arts.

Kano was an educator during this essential time period. He also had an excellent command of English, increasing his understanding of Western ways during his travels. In his journeys abroad, Kano came into constant contact with emerging Western sports—baseball, football, basketball, wrestling, fencing, etc.—and their ideals. Originally, these sports had come about as a way for the Western armies to maintain their physical health. Kano saw value in this, too. He wanted to preserve the timeless qualities of jujutsu—loyalty, discipline, resolve, honor, morality—and discard the traditional qualities in which the martial artist learns techniques to hurt, maim and kill. To do this, his new sport would have to be safe, rewarding and challenging for practitioners. It would also need rules and some method by which to judge performance.

From there, the exact chronology of judo's rule development is difficult to outline, but because of Kano's efforts to develop judo into a sport, we now observe the following:

1. Techniques that might cause serious injuries or are hard to control are not allowed in competition. They include certain leg locks, back locks, finger locks, ankle locks, wrist locks, punches, kicks, knee strikes, elbow strikes, etc. Thus, if these prohibited techniques are used in competition, the offending competitor is penalized by the referee.

2. There is a point system. The person with the highest score at the end of the match wins, unless someone wins by an ippon, which is a full point, or a *hansoku make*, which is a penalty win. There are also lesser scores of wazari, which is a half point, or a yuko, which is a superior advantage point. These scores are accumulated for pins, chokes and armbars.

3. Originally, contest times were indefinite and the winner was usually the last person standing. Gradually, time limits were instituted. They are currently five minutes long. An ippon or hansoku make ends the match instantly. Otherwise, the match continues until the end of five minutes. If the scores are even, the match can be extended into what's called a golden score time. The first point earned wins the match or the first penalty incurred loses the match.

As of 2010, there are two major ways to win a tournament match. The preferred method is to score by either a throw, pin, joint lock, choke or decision win by the referee over the opponent. The other way to win is by forcing your opponent into penalty situations.

True/False

1. *Jujutsu* was used originally to maim or kill the opponent.

2. Judo is an Olympic sport that preserves the finer qualities of the martial arts.

3. To qualify as a sport, judo had to keep safety in mind.

4. Jigoro Kano injected the idea of sports into Japanese martial arts.

5. *Ukemi* or the art of falling was a factor in changing judo into a sport.

Answers: 1.t, 2.t, 3.t, 4.t, 5.t

Ukemi

To make judo techniques safe to practice, Kano included falling techniques in his new curriculum. He took these falling techniques from two schools of jujutsu: *kito ryu* and *tenshin shinryo ryu*. Ukemi helps condition students to instinctively fall into positions that avoid serious injury when they hit the mat. Today, ukemi is one of the first things that most judoka learn and is integral to any *judoka*'s training.

Photo by Eric Nishioka

These *judoka* are practicing *ukemi*, which are techniques for falling safely. They allow judo practitioners the ability to get thrown to the ground and recover quickly to continue their practice.

Scoring by Techniques

In regards to scoring, you can win by submissions or points. You score with a submission if your opponent taps twice; this wins you the match. If your opponent doesn't tap twice, then the match continues.

In regards to points, there are three ways to be awarded points as the result of a throw. You are awarded one point, or ippon, if you perform a picture-perfect throw on your opponent with speed, force and control that lands him squarely on his back. If any of the mentioned criteria are missing in the throw, the referee may award you a half point, or wazari, instead. Think of the ippon as the reward for a perfect throw whereas the wazari is for an almost-perfect throw. The third score is a yuko and has no specific numerical value. Instead, it is known as a superior advantage point, and no amount of yuko can supersede a wazari. A yuko is given when the opponent lands on his side or when two of the elements of an ippon-worthy throw are missing. These scores are largely judgment calls from trained referees.

Scoring for *osaekomi waza*, which is a category of pinning techniques, is determined by the amount of time the opponent is being pinned. (The Japanese word *osae* means to press or hold down.) Osaekomi waza techniques suggest a vertical structure in which one competitor is over the other. In judo, this means the person doing the pinning should be facing downward while the opponent is facing upward. The attacking competitor must not have any part of his body entwined in the defender's legs or the pin isn't valid. Once the referee announces osaekomi (hold down), the timer commences and is valid for as long as any part of the competitor—the person doing the pinning or the person being pinned—remains in contact with the contest area. To receive an ippon, you must hold the opponent down for at least 25 seconds. Should the opponent escape before the 25 seconds is up but after 20 seconds has gone by, the referee will probably award a wazari score. A pin that lasts only 15 to 19 seconds warrants a yuko score.

Osaekomi waza are pinning techniques that are the basis for groundwork. Here, a judoka pins his opponent down with a modified *kata gatame* or shoulder-hold pin.

Joint locks or *kansetsu waza* may be taken only on the elbow joint. Since this is a submission hold, the opponent has the option of tapping twice on the competitor rendering the joint lock or tapping on the mat surface. The opponent can tap with his hands, feet or head while making a sound suggestive of submission. The competitor can also execute *waki gatame* armbars as long as he remains standing or if he initiates it on the ground. He is prohibited from executing an armbar from a standing position and then taking the opponent instantly to the ground. This is because it doesn't give the opponent time to submit; he can't tap out. Note: Generally, a joint lock leads to a dislocated arm if the opponent doesn't tap.

Strangulation techniques or *shime waza* cut off the blood supply to the brain, rendering the opponent unconscious. They are a type of submission technique. In judo, this means that the competitor chokes out the opponent until he submits by tapping twice. Should the opponent not tap, he could lose consciousness. If that happens, the competitor merely releases the choke. Blood should reflow back to the opponent's brain and consciousness will return, even without the use of resuscitation techniques. Studies at the Kodokan Judo Institute in Tokyo, which is the most prestigious judo institution in the world, indicate that chokes aren't dangerous if held for short periods of time. This could be anywhere from five to 10 seconds. However, caution is advised no matter what. (Note: If the opponent passes out without tapping, he is officially eliminated from the rest of tournament.)

Decision wins at the end of a five-minute match are awarded to the person having the highest score. However, not all scores are created equal. A wazari can only be surpassed by another wazari. This means that even if the opponent has scored two, three or even seven yuko, he won't be awarded the win as long as the competitor has a wazari. If the decision is based on penalties, then the person with the fewest minor infractions wins.

After you execute a *shime waza*, your opponent needs to tap twice. Only then will the referee confer the win on you.

POINTS	=	PENALTIES
---------	=	**Freebie Shido**
Yuko	=	**Second Shido**
Wazari	=	**Third Shido**
Ippon	=	**Fourth Shido** (also known as *hansoku make*)

Scoring by Penalties

The other way to win a tournament match is by causing the opponent to accumulate penalties. This is a very effective strategy. For example, during the 1988 Olympics in South Korea, Brazilian fighter Aurelio Miguel accomplished what no other fighter had done before or has done since. He won by guile. He caused all of his opponents to make costly mistakes for which they were penalized by referees. Without executing a single throw, Miguel became the Olympic gold medalist. However, just because Miguel opted to use the rules to his advantage didn't mean he wasn't capable of throwing his opponents. And while some may criticize his method of winning, Miguel did win, and a champion judoka uses all available methods of winning, as allowed by the rules.

So what penalties should you understand in order to maximize your chances of winning? Let's consider penalties through three categories: serious, slight and unwritten.

Grave or serious infringements are penalties incurred when a competitor uses a technique that may cause injury or is against the spirit of the sport. Some of the more common ones include:

1. head diving the opponent in order to execute a throw
2. winding your leg around the opponent's leg and then throwing him backward, such as with an *ouchi gari*
3. derogatory gestures or remarks
4. joint locks to body parts other than the elbow
5. reaping back into the supporting leg of the opponent
6. lifting and smashing while the opponent is in the guard position
7. falling backward while the opponent is on your back
8. wearing any hard or metallic objects
9. directly grabbing below the waist with the hands

The right natural grip is done by gripping the opponent's left collar with the right hand and right sleeve with the left hand. Anything other than this grip can incur a *shido*.

Any of these penalties can eliminate you not only from the match but in some cases from the entire tournament. These penalties are referred to as "direct hansoku make." Think of them like the ippon of penalties.

Slight infringements are penalties given to offending players who prevent the match from proceeding in general or proceeding fairly. These are called *shido,* and shido don't have a numerical value so much as a cumulative one. The first shido you earn is considered "free." The second is equal to a yuko. The third is equal to a wazari. The fourth is equal to an ippon. This means that if you accumulate four shido, you lose the match.

Golden Score Shido

Say you have two competitors: Takashi and James. Takashi incurs one *shido* during the five-minute round. James doesn't manage to score any points. According to the rules, they are tied because Takashi's shido is a freebie. The two competitors now go into overtime. If Takashi incurs another shido, he loses. If James incurs a shido, the match still continues. This is because now James has a freebie. Takashi would need James to incur a second shido before James could lose the match. If neither side scores in the appointed overtime, the referees will decide.

The most common shido given is the "noncombativity" ruling. The referee will make this call if no appreciable technique has been executed after 25 seconds. To avoid this penalty, you may have to feign a low-risk attack, such as *harai goshi* or *kouchi gari*—anything that will throw the opponent off-balance but not get you into a tight spot. However, if there is no appreciable result, the feigning competitor will receive a "false attack" penalty. This penalty is perhaps the second or third most given penalty in tournament matches.

Another common slight infringement is when you assume defensive posture. This is when you assume an excessively defensive attitude, such as avoiding a grip or bending way over with extended arms. Usually, defensive competitors are trying to avoid being thrown and are characterized by stiff arms and excessively bent-over positions. Generally, you can avoid this penalty by remaining upright and looking aggressive. It's just a matter of not getting overwhelmed by your situation.

Judo has a lot of rules, but there is one in particular that can seem negligible. It can also incur you a shido if you're unaware of it. That rule is that you can't do anything that is against the spirit of judo. It's an ambiguous rule that is open to and has received wide interpretation. Your concern is how the referee or judges interpret it. For example, they could give you shido for any of the following: not bowing correctly, entering the competition area without respect, having an untidy appearance, etc. This rule could also be used by officials to benefit hometown favorites. That's why it's a good idea to be friendly, respectful and aware of the rules.

True/False

1. The two major categories of scoring are by techniques and by penalties.

2. The three elements for scoring an *ippon* with a throw are control, force, and the opponent must land largely on his back.

3. An *osae* that lasts 19 seconds will earn the attacking competitor a *wazari.*

4. The defending competitor will tap twice to signify his or her submission, such as in choking, joint-lock and hold-down situations.

5. The most common penalty is for noncombativity.

Answers: 1.T, 2.T, 3.F, 4.T, 5.T

Using the Rules to Your Advantage

There is no definitive list of advanced judo tactics to learn because they don't have specific names like *osoto gari* and seoinage. Bending tournament rules to your advantage is about awareness of the finer points of a competition. You need to learn the feeling of a match. You must understand how the timing, environment and equipment of a tournament can affect your chances of success. In contrast to traditional techniques, the path to understanding and studying advanced judo tactics is more nebulous. But tactics are still as important as techniques because what else are they but tools that help you win?

Consider the following ways in which to use advanced judo tactics:

1. Competitor A has three shido against him while Competitor B has two shido against him. There are more than two minutes left in the match. Competitor B decides to think tactically because the competitors will go into overtime if Competitor B earns another shido. However, Competitor B can win if he maintains the status quo or causes Competitor A to incur another penalty. So what does Competitor B do? He uses a series of attacks based on the 25-second rule: off-the-grip attacks, low-risk attacks, one-handed judo, proper false attacks, etc., to kill time until the end of the match. Even if both competitors each earn another shido, Competitor B still will come out ahead.

2. This time Competitor B figures out that Competitor A is a slow starter. Because of this, Competitor A receives a penalty early on in the match, which stresses her out. Competitor B decides to increase her opponent's stress level by using the 25-second rule to score penalties off Competitor A. Competitor B knows that even if she freezes her entries, she'll get a freebie shido while Competitor A gets a second one.

There are many ways to use the rules and your environment to your benefit, and the rest of the chapter will specify some of these scenarios. There are always more; you just have to know how to identify the opportunities.

Low-Risk Attacks

Remember on page 24, the one-year sample strategy talked about low-risk attacks? Low-risk attacks are attacks that you use when you don't want to be penalized for a false attack and/or countered at the same time.

Low-risk attacks are a kind of advanced judo tactic, too. These attacks are very useful when less than two thirds of the match is left and you want to maintain your lead. If you have two minutes left in the match and are ahead by a yuko with no penalties against you, you will need three or four convincing low-risk attacks. What makes them convincing is if your opponent stumbles or is forced off-balance. Your four attacks should be done approximately every 25 seconds within the remaining two-minute period, which you count mentally or your coach signals to you. If you decide to stall, you probably only need to launch two low-risk attacks. Remember, the first shido is a free one and the second one is scored. So if you have no penalties, it's okay if you incur one shido because it's a freebie.

Here are a few of the suggested throws for low-risk attacks:

1. outside in *sode tsurikomi goshi*
2. ippon seoinage

3. drop ouchi gari

4. an attack that may not score but will off-balance the opponent

The drop seoinage unless well-executed should be avoided. It is one of the most penalized techniques for false attacks. This is when you grip the opponent's judogi with two hands, making it easier for the opponent to resist your grip. When you drop to the floor, the opponent may remain standing and this will incur you a shido for not off-balancing him.

Although foot techniques are encouraged, they are rarely credited as an attack because they rarely knock the opponent off-balance and are more likely to be countered. When you are ahead, you don't want to take any unnecessary chances.

Gauging Match Time

To keep time in a match, you have to learn how to gauge it. How else would you execute the 25-second rule during the last half of a round?

In a match, you have five minutes to keep track of, and they can seem to go by faster or slower depending on whether you have to catch up or maintain the lead. While beginners often lose themselves inside the match, the advanced player has to be aware of how much time is left in the match even under stressful conditions. Most people think that the ring that signals the end of a five-minute match is all they need, but is it enough?

Consider this experiment in which a friend times you: After he or she says, "Go," you try to guess when the minute is up. The point of the exercise is to help you get the feel for how long a minute is. The more you practice it, the closer you should get to saying "Stop" right on time.

It's very important to understand the length of a minute in judo. Consider this variation of the same experiment under stress: Your friend with the timer says, "Go." Then he yells, "STOP!" whenever he feels like it. You need to know where you are in the minute. Will you know? Or will you be too jarred by the "STOP!" to answer?

Now, consider the half minute. This is a very important amount of time in a match because you must apply a technique every 25 to 30 seconds. If you don't, you'll be penalized. But get this: The opponent needs to apply a technique every 25 to 30 seconds, too!

So here's a neat trick:

You're in a match and ahead by a yuko. You know that you will be penalized for noncombativity so you establish a grip, which takes five to 10 seconds. In attacking, this means the opponent has five to 10 seconds of noncombativity against him on the clock. You push your opponent, preventing him from making an attack, with advanced tactics. To the referees, it looks like you're being very aggressive whereas the opponent looks like he is being very defensive. When 25 seconds are up, the opponent will incur a shido penalty. By using several advanced tactics in conjunction with your awareness of time, you cause the opponent to step into a penalty trap. (The best time to do this is after the free penalty has already been given to the opponent or near the end of the match to secure a penalty win.)

Execute a Proper False Attack

As mentioned earlier in the chapter, a false attack incurs a penalty if no appreciable and aggressive technique has been applied to stumble or off-balance the opponent. A false-attack penalty earns you a shido.

This can be a big deal. For example, in the 1996 Olympics, World Champion Ryoko Tamura of Japan was heavily favored to win in the final match against Kye Sun-Hui of North Korea. During the match, Tamura applied a drop seoinage near the edge of the mat, but unfortunately, her opponent stood upright, unfettered by the attempt. For some reason, Tamura stopped her attack. Perhaps she thought she might go outside the mat or perhaps she sensed that it was futile to use her energy up on a failed attempt. Whatever the reason, Tamura incurred a shido because she failed to off-balance her opponent. After that, Tamura couldn't regain her lead and lost what could have been her first-ever gold medal. It would be another four years before she'd get the chance to strike gold again.

So, what happened? Tamura incurred a false-attack penalty because she entered into a technique that didn't break Kye Sun-Hui's balance. Here are some things Tamura could have done tactically to avoid the penalty:

1. If your attack fails, do not stop! Continue to pull even with one hand and try to tilt the opponent's posture. Even if the opponent remains upright, continue to curl as if to throw him. If you don't, you can argue: "Had I not released the opponent's judogi, he might have gone over."

2. If you fail in your throw, don't stop! Instead, quickly proceed to attack with a different throw, even if it's in a different direction. Just don't stop!

3. If your attempt fails and you are near an arm, foot or toe, immediately grab it and pull it down for *ne waza*. You want to at least look as if you are trying to do so.

Of course, there may be more options, but the main thing to remember is to not stop your attack. You want to continue to look active in trying to off-balance the opponent somehow.

The responses listed above just have to become practiced and instinctive. Like traditional techniques, they must be practiced with uchikomi entry drills because they help ingrain techniques into your nerves and muscles. Moreover, if done correctly a proper false attack may score you a point, which means for once it won't be an oxymoron. Remember, every little advantage helps.

Pacing

Smart players know how to change the pace of their match. If a smart player sees that his opponent prefers to fight at a fast pace, then the smart player will slow down. Or if the opponent is slow, the smart judoka will keep him off-balance by stepping up the action. Sometimes smart players change pace not as a matter of comfort but as a matter of necessity. They may feel pressure to resort to this tactic if they're behind and have little time to catch up.

Slow the pace. Walk slower. Move faster. Grip faster. Press the opponent to the edge. Control the gauging arm. Keep the opponent off-balance and know how best to work your five-minute match to fit your conditions.

For some unknown reason, competitors who score early in the match also become anxious early in the match. Rather than pacing themselves, they fire technique after technique. They're using all their energy not trying to *throw* but trying to run out the clock so that their opponent is unable to get in a throw and possibly take away the lead. Big mistake. When you expend too much energy, you get tired. When that happens, you lose your ability to defend yourself. This allows the fresher opponent to get in a good ippon throw later in the match, and guess what? Game over!

Coaches and athletes need to know their game and how to play it right. Otherwise, you could end up tired like Sam from the chapter introduction, who was running out of steam while trying to maintain the lead. (This is actually a common error made by American judoka.) Of course, if you have superior technique over your opponent and can throw him or her, then you're fine. But if not, you'll need to rely on your strength and conditioning to outlast your opponent. In doing so, you'll expend more energy, and you only have a limited supply. After all, glycogen, which are your energy stores, can be depleted in about 10 seconds or less. In other words, you won't be able to do a second or third 100-yard dash at the same performance level as the first. You'll be out of gas. Judo has the same problem: If you use up your glycogen stores in the first 10 seconds, how do you contend with the remaining 4 minutes and 50 seconds of the match?

The solution is preparation. Many judo clubs practice five-minute interval randori sessions. That is, they change partners every five minutes. The purpose of these quickfire randori sessions is to develop the judoka's feel for a five-minute workout. During these spans, you should mimic contest situations as closely as possible and pay attention to how you utilize your energy. Pay particular attention to what a five-minute timespan feels like. Practice and be able to implement many of the tactics mentioned in this chapter. You don't need to practice all of them, but you should incorporate the ones that fit your style and needs.

Using Your Borders

Contest areas are a minimum of 8-by-8 meters, but competitors tend to rarely use the middle of the mat. In fact, the better competitor knows how to use the edges to his tactical advantage. Here are a few ideas to get you started on thinking not only about the line but on it:

1. If your opponent is better than you in ne waza, it is better to be by the edge of the mat than in the center of it. This is because you'll be in less danger of wriggling to the outside, losing contact with the contest area and breaking the hold down.

2. Against weaker players, consider backing them up to the edge for added pressure. Because their attention will be split between not stepping out and your possible attack, you will have the advantage.

3. Against stronger players, you can use pressure as well, especially if you have been practicing and drilling these border situations and your opponent hasn't. As in the situation described at the beginning of this chapter, you don't want to be Karla; you want the other guy to be Karla.

4. Some players will move to your right or left when you need them to move in the opposite direction in order to execute your throw. Move them into a corner and block the side opposite of where you want them to move. They will then move in the opposite direction of where you are standing in the way.

Currently, a technique started from within the contest area, even though it flows to the outside, will count. At one time, penalties were assessed even when an attacker stepped out while attempting a throw much less just stepping outside the contest area. This is no longer a worry unless a contestant continually goes to the outside as a defensive maneuver.

Uniforms

At the beginning of the chapter, Julio, the judoka from the Dominican Republic, made the mistake of buying a lightweight and single-weave gi for his competition. Without even realizing it, Julio had made an error that probably cost him the tournament. Too often, competitors buy the wrong gi just because they don't know any better. What are the consequences of buying the wrong gi? Well, let's say you live in North Carolina and plan to go to a tournament in Los Angeles. For the trip, you invest in extra practice times and training, airfare, hotels, rental cars, etc. To save a few bucks you,

like Julio, decide to buy a cheap gi that is lightweight and easy to pack. However, because of your decision, your opponent, who is wearing a heavier and double-weave gi, is able to take you out in the first match. All your investments don't mean anything now.

The blue-belt competitor is at an obvious disadvantage because he is wearing an oversize uniform. His opponent can easily grip and maneuver him into vulnerable positions.

So what does it mean to wear the proper uniform? First, always stay within the rules; they are very clear on uniform guidelines. But in staying in the rules, you don't have to give your potential opponent an advantage. A heavier and double-weave gi is harder and thicker for the opponent to handle. To see what that means, test it out. Grip a single-weave uniform by the sleeve and have your partner try to break your grip. Then grip a double-weave uniform and have your training partner try to break your grip. He should be able to break your grip much more easily with a double-weave gi.

Note: All judogi will be measured with a *sokuteiki*—the International Judo Federation approved gi-measuring device—before the tournament. As of summer 2010, many competitions require competitors to use only IJF-approved judogi.

Also make sure that your judogi fits correctly. If it is too large or too small, get it properly tailored. Have no doubt that an oversize single-weave judogi will give your opponent a larger area in which to grip you, whereas a proper fitting double-weave judogi will minimize his gripping control.

For youngsters, adhering to this tactic might not be as important as it is for other serious judoka. The reason is that young judoka are still growing and proper gi are expensive, ranging from $150 to $200. In addition to that, any serious judoka needs a blue and white gi. So in the end, coaches and parents need to decide what's more important for the young competitor—gaining a tactical edge or developing a sense of enjoyment for good techniques and judo movements. Forcing young champions to be aware of the details so early on may cause them to burn out and decide against continuing in high-pressured judo life as adults. It's just something to think about.

Mat Surfaces

Legendary swordsman Miyamoto Musashi was said to have been challenged to do battle with 15 to 20 opponents at one time. To prepare for his match prior to the engagement, Musashi went to the site to study the terrain. He discovered that the match area was bordered by a rice field with soggy moats; there were narrow bridges built through the field so farmers wouldn't have to step in the mud. Musashi used this information to win his fight. How? Instead of fighting his multiple opponents on an open and dry field, Musashi took the fight into the rice fields. Musashi held his ground on the bridges, which would only allow one to two opponents to attack the double-sword-wielding Musashi at once. The other opponents had to slog their way through the mud, making their movements slow enough that Musashi was able to cut them down, too.

How does this apply to judo competition? Easy—know your environment and what it feels like.

In the United States, judoka practice on many different mat surfaces—horse hair, composite, wrestling mats, Japanese tatami, canvas-covered mats and European tatami. Each of these mats has a different surface feel. Some feel more textured and thus are not as fast to move on. Some feel smoother, so you move more quickly. Some feel sticky, slick, etc. It is best to step on the mat before a competition and get used to the surface. Sometimes this mental awareness is enough to give you the advantage in a competition. After all, if your dojo trains on wrestling mats and now you're on Japanese straw mats, you may need to make some mental adjustments before stepping on the mat for a match.

First Grip

Until the 1960s, judoka didn't think much about gripping skills. Then the former USSR judo team entered the Olympics and brought *sambo*-wrestling grips into the tournament. The team's many victories because of the grips stunned the judo world. Today, understanding gripping skills is a must, and this is especially true at higher levels of competition.

Former national judo champion Kari Gabriel coaches her competitor to grip his opponent.

One of the most common lessons that students learn in beginning judo is to get the first grip possible. In advanced judo, getting the first grip becomes more difficult to accomplish because it gives the gripper a decided advantage. The first person to grip is the competitor who gets to dictate the direction of play. If you grip first, then the opponent has to react. You pull, he will pull. The first grip is like playing "King of the Mountain." The first to the top is better able to maintain that top position.

The thing to remember about the first grip is that in many ways, we're referring to the first good grip or dominant grip that allows a competitor a better position in which to attack. So this means that the first grip isn't necessarily the "first grip" of the entire match. It is the first grip in the current tussle that you find yourself in with your opponent.

Because the first grip gives the competitor control over the person who doesn't have a grip, you need to do something with that grip in order to stabilize the situation. If you don't, then your opponent will counter and turn you into the defender.

There are many different methods of getting the first grip. Here are a few suggestions to get you started:

1. ***Isolate the grip:*** This is where both your hands are in front and you are concentrating on the opponent's oncoming arm. As it comes forward, you catch it with both hands from below. Once isolated, pull it downward and secure it with your rear hand. Now quickly reach for

the lapel with your lead hand. For grips that come in at a low angle, one hand goes under and the other goes over the opponent's gripping arm. As his grip is about to tighten up, place your weight over your extended arm and shove downward and away.

2. *Fluffing-up grip:* This technique is done against a person who has his judogi tucked tightly into his belt. Reaching for a judogi in this condition may be risky because your arm is extended, thus allowing the opponent to grip you. Therefore, draw the opponent's judogi out of the belt through a series of quick pecking-type maneuvers with your lead hand and far out enough to get a grip on it.

3. *Cross grip:* Because the left lapel is usually crossed over the right, a tightly tucked-in judogi may be difficult to grip with your lead right hand because the label faces in the same direction in which your fingers are coming into grip. If you swipe across in the opposite direction with the left hand, you can insert your fingers because the right lapel's positioning is easier to hook. Once gripped, the judogi may be pulled out and quickly transferred to the other hand. In some cases in which there has been some preparation, a technique may be executed from this grip even without switching grips—perhaps an inside or outside seoinage. Also, while some competitors can maintain and execute throws from the cross grip, it is generally not advised. If you hold it for more than five seconds, you may incur a penalty, so once the judogi has been pulled out enough to grasp, grab it.

4. *Elbow-offering grip:* Extend your lead elbow to offer your opponent an elbow grip. Once he takes it, rotate your elbow and upper body counterclockwise. Your rear hand simultaneously will be moving clockwise to intercept the opponent's lead-hand grip—which hand the opponent uses depends on which arm you offer him. Once your rear-hand grip is secure, quickly reverse the direction of your hands in a scissoring-type motion. Your rear hand continues to pull while your lead hand and arm should be free to assume a grip around the backside of the opponent's uniform. This grip is ideal for a lateral direction *sumi-gaeshi.* Many of these nontraditional gripping techniques, such as cross grip and elbow-offering grip, must be followed up with a technique within five seconds or else you may be penalized with a shido.

Isolate the Grip No. 1

1: Tori (left) stands with both hands in front of him. Uke is contemplating whether to grasp tori's arm.

2: As uke reaches for tori's collar, tori uses both hands to form a U shape under uke's incoming arm.

3: Tori shoves uke's arm up and away, and at the same time, he arches and pulls backward to isolate the grip.

Isolate the Grip No. 2

1: As uke (right) is about to grasp tori's collar, tori intercepts uke's right hand. The tori grips with his right hand from above and his left hand from below.

2: Tori shoves uke's arm down and away.

3: Once he has pushed uke's incoming arm down, tori pulls up with his right hand to grip uke's left collar.

Fluffing-Up the Grip

1: Uke's judogi is neatly tucked into his belt. Tori (left) wants to get hold of it so he will fluff up the grip.

2-5: Running your eyes over these four pictures, you will see how tori uses pecking maneuvers to progressively pull out the opponent's judogi until he can get a grip.

Cross Grip

1: Tori (left) will execute a cross grip by reaching across and grasping uke's left lapel with his left hand.

2: The cross grip in action is pictured here. Note how tori's hands cross over the midline of uke's body in order to grip the judogi rather than just gripping from the front. Tori's right hand is to the opponent's left side, and tori's left hand is to the opponent's right side.

Elbow-Offering Grip

1: Tori (right) extends his elbow forward, and uke takes the grip.

2: Tori now shoves his gripped elbow forward while rotating his body counterclockwise. The action extends uke's arm and body forward, too.

3: With uke's arm forward, tori grabs uke's sleeve. Tori will rip backward while pulling uke's sleeve forward in a shearing action with his right elbow. This action will release uke's grasp of tori's elbow.

4: With his elbow and arm free, tori reaches across uke's back to take a back cross grip. There are throws that can be executed from this position, but because it is a cross grip, tori's attempt must be made within five seconds or else he may risk a penalty.

While it is important to get a grip, it is even more important to do something with the grip once you have it. Hopefully it will be to attack. In many instances getting a grip is for defensive purposes. It is the stellar athlete who gets a grip to be on the offensive. During practice it is a good idea to see how quickly you can identify an opening and attack. Once you get your grip, your opponent will sense that he is in danger and will make quick adjustments. You need to act as quickly as possible allowing little time to build a tolerance to your technique.

Breaking a Grip

Breaking a grip is a different action from taking or isolating a grip. Instead, it is about avoiding being grabbed at all. You break the grip in order to spoil the opponent's attempt to throw you.

If you have been studying your opponent, you should know what grips he or she takes when executing favorite moves. If you have practiced with the individual, you should be able to sense an impending attack when he or she takes a particular grip. Just as you sense this feeling, you should try to break off any grip he or she has on you.

Photo by Pamela Yamane, Kaizen Concepts

One of the best times to break a grip is just as the opponent is about to get one. One method is to use both hands on his or her reaching right hand from below. As the grip is being taken, form a U shape with both hands and catch the arm near the wrist, then give a quick pump upward and towards your opponent. You should practice this over and over, feeling the opponent's fingers release as you push away with your arms and jerk your upper body backwards at the same time.

If you have gone against your opponent before and had a difficult time with certain grips, you should have a friend mimic the grip and drill you to break the grip or at least build a tolerance for the grip.

The blue gi competitor has come up from under his opponent's arm just as the opponent was about to tighten his grip.

Breaking the Grip

1: Uke (right) grips tori's sleeve from below.

2: Tori rotates his left hand over uke's wrist to tighten and twist the judogi. At the same time, tori brings his right hand over uke's wrist to push it downward.

3: With a quick push down and away with his right hand and up and back with his left hand, tori breaks the grip.

4: Now he's free to begin again and get the first grip.

Isolating the Grip

1: The white-judogi tori is anticipating a collar grip by his uke in the blue judogi.

2: Uke shoots his hand forward in an effort to grab tori's left-side collar. But tori is ready; he brings his hands up in a U shape underneath uke's extended arm.

3: Before uke can secure a good grip, tori snaps away uke's hand with a quick shove and at the same time arches backward to avoid uke's grasp.

Leg Release

1: Uke (left) has gripped tori, but tori can't seem to get a grip on uke's judogi.

2: Tori brings his knee up high enough so he can grab or place his hand on the side of his raised leg.

3: With a quick stomping motion, tori kicks backward while maintaining a grip on that leg. The force of the kicking leg should be enough to free tori from uke's grip.

High-Grip Escape

1: The high-grip escape is executed while uke (left) is taking a grip.

2: As uke's arm is about to grip behind tori's neck, tori ducks his head slightly and places his right hand behind the elbow of uke's gripping arm.

3: Using his arm to shove the opponent's arm across and counterclockwise, tori rotates his body and breaks the grip.

Instant Attacks

In Japanese fencing there is a saying that kendo practitioners follow called "*sen no sen*" or "line of a line." The aphorism means that when an attacker is about to attack you should preempt it by taking the offensive yourself and taking away the attacker's line of attack. It's very similar to what Bruce Lee taught—your perfect defense is an offensive hit.

In judo, the same lines of thought apply. If you can grip and go on an off-the-grip attack, that means you get a grip on the opponent and attack at the same time. Imagine you are ahead by a yuko with a minute left in the match. The opponent is desperate to attack, but every time he tries, you attack first by taking a grip or keeping up a constant barrage that disallows any attack on his part. If you can maintain your focus and attack off the grip, who do you think will win?

Let's reconsider that match. You now have more than a minute left and you want to use the preemptive grip-and-go tactic to trick your opponent into a penalty or maintain your lead. You slow your pace suddenly before quickly shifting into a burst of grip-and-go attacks. You slow down again and mind your time. You unleash another burst of grip-and-go attacks. When doing this, be mindful of your cardiovascular abilities and anaerobic threshold.

Somewhat similar to the preemptive attack is the off-the-grip attack. This is a gutsy move because your plan is to attack just after the referee says, "*Hajime.*" This is best done at the beginning of the match but may also be done during the match, as it is about to resume. It's just, "Hajime," grab and go!

Many competitors don't expect an off-the-grip attack. Instead, they expect the usual sequence: 1) get a grip, 2) jockey for position, 3) find an opening, and 4) attack. By executing an off-the-grip attack, you eliminate steps two and three—you just grab and attack.

On the timer in the background, you can see that the competitors are just seven seconds into the match. However, the blue competitor has unleashed an *osoto gari* on the white competitor who was expecting to fight a five-minute match.

The way to first practice this is to apply the tactic to a willing training partner. See how it feels. If it feels right, speed up your pacing and try it in real time. To really get used to the tactic, do 100 or so entry drills.

The following are a few suggestions to practice your instant attacks. Remember that you should be focused on throwing the instant you take a grip because it will increase your chances of winning. The recommendations are:

1. *de ashi barai*
2. ippon seoinage
3. sode tsurikomi goshi
4. *morote seoinage*

5. ouchi gari

6. soto makikomi

One-Handed Judo

In the 1996 Olympics, Udo Quellmalz of Germany fought Yukimasa Nakamura of Japan in the finals. Out of the entire five-minute match, Quellmalz and Nakamura were tied up for less than a half minute. They gripped each other with only one hand, and each sporadically attacked with foot techniques. Finally, Quellmalz executed a kouchi gari and Nakamura had to twist to his stomach to avoid being thrown to the back and scored on. At the end of the match, the decision win went to Quellmalz because he had achieved the only knockdown close to any kind of possible score. Throughout the five-minute match, Quellmalz and Nakamura had actually only engaged in about 18 seconds of two-handed judo.

Many have speculated that had Nakamura been fighting in a match where he could use his usual two-handed gripping style, he probably would have won. Quellmalz, however, was aware of his opponent's strong two-handed game. The German judoka had drilled and practiced one-handed judo because he knew he would have a better chance of fighting Nakamura in a style that was unfamiliar to the Japanese competitor. In the end, Quellmalz's strategy and tactics worked—he got the gold medal and Nakamura didn't.

One-handed judo can give you that same opportunity, especially if you have practiced it, when you need time to get used to your opponent's style or if your opponent is stronger than you. A cautionary point however: Because one-handed judo is a defensive tactic, you need to look aggressive or else you'll be penalized a shido. You might incur a noncombativity shido because you haven't made a substantial attack within 25 seconds. You could also incur a false-attack penalty if you don't cause your opponent to at least stumble within every 25-second period.

It's twice as hard to enter into a throw when your opponent is holding you with two arms. Therefore, it's better to attack when the opponent is only gripping you with one hand. This is also why one-handed judo is an unexpected tactic.

There are a few judoka who can do one-handed judo effectively. It is an unnatural style of judo to many practitioners but if done correctly, it can be a powerful tool in your arsenal. As with anything, it just takes practice.

Proper Frame of Mind

The ancient Japanese warrior Minamoto Yoritomo once stated that the outcome of a battle is determined by the preparation one has invested. To worry excessively over the possible outcome is to drain energy.

While such an idea may seem to be more strategic in nature, it should be part of your tactics to

Photo by Pamela Yamane, Kaizen Concepts

With the proper mind-set, you'll defend when attacked, attack when there is an opening and alternate between these two responses when appropriate. There will be no other space in your mind for doubt. You'll seize the moment.

mentally fight the match and review all that you have done to prepare before you even step on the mat. If done correctly, it should psych you up physically. You are there. Now, fight!

Here are a few suggestions to mentally prepare:

1. Go over your competitor profiles (see Chapter 5) and see if you have made the necessary adjustments during practice sessions to meet the demands of the opponents. That means knowing his or her style and adjusting yours to neutralize it. Do you have a plan of attack and a couple of backups? Are you ready muscularly, cardiovascularly, technically, tactically?

2. Go over your logbook to rekindle important thoughts and ideas that may aid you.

3. Spend some time practicing meditation and relaxation techniques. Get plenty of rest and sleep but avoid sleeping pills. Taking in a movie or watching television will give your mind a rest from the nervous thoughts of tomorrow's tournament and its outcome.

Tomorrow will come and go. It will have an outcome, a small part of which is a result of random luck and a large part of which is determined by your physical preparation. How did you prepare for this focused moment in time? As you step onto the mat, all systems must say, "Go!"

True/False

1. The type of uniform you wear doesn't matter as long as you have good techniques.

2. It is always best not to use nontraditional grips because penalties are always applied.

3. The object of getting a grip should be to throw the opponent.

4. Better contestants know how to not only gauge their time but also what to do within the time allotted.

5. Low-risk attacks, grip breaking, proper false attacks, one-handed judo, mat work and using the line are means of controlling the lead.

Answers: 1.f, 2.f, 3.t, 4.t, 5.t

Chapter Review

1. In what ways did Jigoro Kano transform judo into a sport?

2. Describe the three scores that may be awarded in a match for techniques executed.

3. Describe the differences between serious and slight infringements.

4. Discuss the importance of a proper-fitting judogi and how that affects gripping techniques.

5. You are a coach and your student is ahead by a yuko. There is a minute left in the match. What preparations have you made at the dojo that may make the difference in the outcome of this match? Discuss.

"In today's judo, you can't go very far with just one or two techniques."

—Jimmy Pedro, two-time judo bronze medalist, judo coach

A Family of Techniques

CHAPTER FOUR
A Family of Techniques

A competitor named Kiyoshi believed that a judoka needed a favorite technique, which is a technique that works no matter what defense your opponent might choose. For Kiyoshi, that was his seoinage. Whenever he executed that shoulder throw in the dojo, his training partner would be easily brought to the ground. The more Kiyoshi practiced that throw, the better his timing got, too.

It was all so simple—move opponent to the right, swing your left foot in a counterclockwise motion, move right elbow across the opponent's chest and under his armpit. It was like magic.

Then Kiyoshi met up with his old tournament opponent Jimmy. In previous years, Kiyoshi was always able to get his hands on Jimmy to move him right. This time, Jimmy moved in the wrong direction for Kiyoshi. Instead of moving right so that Kiyoshi could throw him, Jimmy moved left. Kiyoshi was flustered by this unexpected turn of events.

Jimmy's first attack scored him a yuko with a left ouchi gari. Then, in quick succession, Jimmy applied a second ouchi gari to a kouchi gari that twisted Kiyoshi to his belly and to the floor. Kiyoshi tried to regroup and thought that he should move forward if Jimmy was trying to push him back. He met Jimmy's second kouchi gari with resistance from the front. Jimmy switched his follow-up technique to a frontal assault and scored an ippon with a *tai otoshi*. Kiyoshi was stunned. What happened?

Unbeknownst to Kiyoshi, Jimmy had been dojo-hopping and practicing his family of techniques in different combinations under different conditions with many different partners. Once at home, Jimmy would review his practice and take notes on what worked, what didn't and what needed to be worked on. In addition, Jimmy knew that Kiyoshi expected him to move right. In moving right, Jimmy knew Kiyoshi would execute his favorite technique: a seoinage. What also worked in Jimmy's favor was that Kiyoshi didn't have a well-rounded family of techniques. He had no back-up plan. He had no technique to execute if his opponent moved in another direction. Therefore, what helped Jimmy literally get a drop on his old rival was his attention to cultivating his technical family.

Queries

1. **In judo today, is it difficult to compete with just one favorite technique?**

2. **What is a family of techniques and why is it important to have one?**

3. **How do you go about developing a family of techniques?**

4. **What did Jimmy do that allowed him to neutralize and win over Kiyoshi?**

5. **What types of techniques can best be included in your family of techniques?**

The *uchimata*, as performed in the photo, is one of the most popular techniques executed in tournament judo. Because of that, it is a good idea to consider adding it to your family of techniques.

Photo by Pamela Yamane, Kaizen Concepts

Building a Family of Techniques

Current competitive judo practices involve the use of multiple techniques in order to defeat an opponent. For the most part, the more techniques you can execute at a high degree of excellence, the better your chances of winning. The caveat: trying to learn too many techniques takes too much time and dilutes the quality of the techniques you want in your family. There are at least 67 traditional throws to select from, not counting the variations that may run up to the 200-plus range, and it can take months to learn even one technique well. So, how do we begin to select our family?

In essence, a family of techniques is a group of techniques that help you win competitions. Because you can't learn everything, concentrate on techniques that will help you in the most situations. Well-rounded families of techniques include skills that help you attack in multiple directions, involve mat work, consider standing throws, and can be used in combinations, feints and counters.

To start with, many competitors who come from a recreational judo background generally just piece together throws they've had success with in the past. Or, they might just choose to focus on their favorites, like the *ogoshi* or maybe the *tomoenage*. While that could be a good place to start, the next step is to plan the next step. Meaning, the first technique can be your favorite, but then you need a follow-up technique. This is what you should do to build a family of techniques when training to win.

For example, if your first technique throws the opponent to the right rear, the next technique mastered should be to the left front in the event the opponent opts to go in the opposite direction of the first throw learned. An example of this would be a right osoto gari combined with a left ippon seoinage or a left and right *okuri ashi barai*.

In the initial development of your family of techniques, you may start with your favorite throw. Develop your family from there. Maybe you should add a technique that goes in the opposite direction? After that, add in a technique you can do in combination with both of your other techniques. Just think about how the match between Kiyoshi and Jimmy might have gone differently if Kiyoshi had just practiced a technique that had gone left!

Here are some families of techniques from well-known world champions and Olympic gold medalists. Notice how no one family is the same as the other, but that each champion relies on more than one favorite throw. The families also include combination throws, mat work, etc., because those techniques flow easily from one to the other. The families of these champions are:

Competitor	Family of Techniques
Yasuhiro Yamashita	osoto gari, uchimata, *yoko shiho* gatame, *kami shiho gatame*, *kesa gatame*, *shime waza uhiro*
Tadahiro Nomura	*sode tsurikomi-guruma*, *okuri ashi barai*, seoinage, osoto gari
Peter Seisenbacher	osoto gari, kouchi gari, tai otoshi, *juji gatame*, kesa gatame
AnnMaria De Mars	osoto gari, kouchi gari, juji gatame, kesa gatame
Michael Swain	tai otoshi, ippon seoinage, de ashi barai, ouchi gari
Jimmy Pedro	tai otoshi, ouchi gari, circular *sumi gaeshi*, uchimata, drop kata guruma, juji gatame, osae waza
Ronda Rousey	osoto gari, harai goshi, uchimata, ouchi gari, sode tsurikomi goshi, juji gatame, kesa gatame

Grooming Your Family of Techniques

To decide on their family of techniques, these judoka probably did quite a bit of grooming. Grooming is when a person goes from simple to complex tasks in a graduated and planned progression. Olympic gold medalist Carl Lewis didn't begin running straight from the womb, after all! He crawled, then walked, ran, raced, then won Olympic gold.

In judo, the coach and athlete map out a strategy on how best to get to a goal, which in this case is a family of techniques. The grooming procedure could go something like this:

1. Learn a technique.

2. Learn another.

3. Make a family of techniques.

4. Practice them with a cooperative partner.

5. Practice them with progressively tougher partners.

6. Increase the ratio of successful attempts during each randori session.

7. Build confidence in your ability to work with your family of techniques.

8. Enter minor tournaments.

9. Enter larger tournaments.

The procedure for grooming a family of techniques can be the same as the procedure for grooming one technique, tactic or strategy. Always start with the basics, then build on them to meet the competition's demands.

As discussed in Chapter 2, both the competitor and the coach should keep a record of the competitor's development—what he or she is doing, what adjustments need to be made in the family of techniques, etc.

Still, one must be cautious; some competitors try to skip steps and hurt themselves mentally, if not physically, when faced with an overwhelmingly negative experience. One example is of a promising new brown belt who traveled across the country to compete in a national event, before testing himself locally and regionally. He lasted less than two minutes. The trip cost him close to $800 and he hasn't been seen since. If he had groomed his family of techniques, he would have realized that he wasn't ready or his coach would have probably advised him that he wasn't prepared for the larger competition.

It's best to try things that you are ready for and have a possibility of succeeding at. Take progress one manageable step at a time. It does take time to develop the requisite abilities at higher levels. Success seems to be a better breeder of success so build on successes you are ready for. That's grooming.

The blue belt is surprised by a left-hand seoinage. Because many competitors don't execute left-handed techniques, there are fewer defenses built up against them.

Principle of Primacy

The principle of primacy holds that whatever an individual learns first is usually what he uses as his base of understanding. For example, a left-handed instructor will often find many of his beginning students mimicking his actions with left-handed techniques, even if they are right-handed. This has training implications that coaches should consider.

Why limit the learning of a technique to just one side, usually the right side? Why not teach one technique that moves to the right and another that moves to the left, thereby increasing the competitor's directions of attack? Why not instruct students to attack in a number of directions right from the start? The first technique taught to Johnny Judo could be a right ogoshi and the next one could be a left ippon seoinage. Now Johnny has bilateral alternatives and a bilateral view of judo techniques. The next technique could be a tomoenage followed by an osoto gari. Now it's possible for Johnny to catch his opponent coming forward toward him or trying to escape to the rear.

Even the former U.S. Senator to Colorado and Olympic judoka, Benjamin Nighthorse Campbell, advocated multidirectional uchikomi drills before every *randori* session. As chief instructor of Sacramento Judo Club, he produced several national champions and Olympians with this philosophy, including six-time national champion Jimmy Martin, Grand National champion Doug Nelson and former U.S. world team member Don Matsuda.

Making Your Family of Techniques Flow

Making your family of techniques flow means that you're able to transition smoothly from one technique to another with little to no lag time in between. Ideally, you want combinations that flow from one technique to another in multiple directions. You have a technique like the morote seoinage that goes right and a technique like the ippon seoinage that goes left. If you tried to execute the morote seoinage, your highly-skilled opponent might anticipate it and try to go left instead. However, because you are prepared, you can immediately transition to the left with your ippon seoinage.

So you've taken care of yourself if your opponent moves laterally or if you want to execute a technique laterally. But what if you want to execute a technique that pushes your opponent backwards? You'll need a technique like the ouchi gari. Your highly-skilled opponent might anticipate this and lean forward. In response, you'll be prepared to turn and execute in the opposite direction with a tai otoshi.

As you can see, you need to be able to anticipate the directions that a match might move so that you can choose complementary techniques that work smoothly with each other. With that said, it's important to realize some techniques don't work together. For example, a tomoenage to a seoinage doesn't work because of the time factor. The tomoenage

A wise addition to your family of techniques would be some form of ground work, like a pin, choke or armbar.

Photo by Pamela Yamane, Kaizen Concepts

takes you and your opponent to the ground, but the seoinage is executed from a standing position. It doesn't make sense to pair the two together in a family of techniques because they don't flow well. You want to choose techniques that will "snap" one into the other, like a well-oiled machine. If your opponent pulls, then you push forward with a kouchi gari. As he resists to the front, you react with a tai otoshi or seoinage. You manage to throw him to the floor and are already prepared with your follow up, which is a juji gatame or kesa gatame.

If you have an intricate strategy, then maybe you'll have circular patterns and techniques. Let's say in a match, you have executed a *hiza guruma*, but your opponent whirls around you to avoid it. Now he's behind you. What do you do? You follow up with your circular okuri ashi barai or *oguruma*. Because you've practiced this and prepared these moves in your family, your opponent is probably on the ground now.

Circular-Pattern Attack

1: A good drill to get familiar with is moving in a circular pattern. To begin, tori (right) steps forward with his right foot. He places it slightly in front of uke's feet. This position allows tori to bring his right arm under uke's left arm. Tori's left arm is grasping uke's right arm lightly. Note how tori leans but uke remains upright in posture.

2: Now uke leans forward slightly because tori is gently pulling him forward and clockwise.

3: Tori continues to draw uke clockwise by stepping back with his right foot. Uke cooperates by merely stepping around his left foot.

4: Tori now slightly shifts his right foot clockwise a quarter of a step, as if he were going to continue around with a full step. Uke thinks that they will continue in a circle so he takes a full step clockwise with his left foot.

5: Uke continues his circular journey, but tori's feet stay stable on the ground. He continues to pull uke with his arms to float uke up on his hip, which tori shifts slightly to the right.

6: Once uke is loaded on tori's hip, tori begins to twist his upper body in the opposite direction. With a wave-type action, he throws uke in a counterclockwise direction.

7: Tori accomplishes the throw. Note: After you are used to the entry rhythm, the pattern will feel like a dance, but with the only difference being that there is a throw at the end of the steps.

Of course, no high-level competitor should go without fakes and counterattacks in his arsenal. Nor should serious competitors and coaches forget about transitional combinations, like moving from a standing position to the mat. However, combinations alone don't make up your family of techniques, and much will depend on the personal likes and dislikes of the competitor as well as his or her ability to execute the techniques. Ideally, you want an attack pattern for every direction you can move on the mat, although this takes time to develop. That's why you need to keep a record of your successes and failures.

Counterattacks

Counterattacks exemplify one of the principles of judo. The principle describes how the judoka gives way to an oncoming force of seven and adds his or her own force of three in the same direction as the oncoming force. This brings the judoka's total force to 10 and helps him or her overcome the opponent.

Counterattacks should be in everyone's family of techniques because they require little energy and come in handy if the opponent is behind in points, tired or overextending him or herself. The hardest thing to learn about counterattacks is the sixth sense you need to know when the opponent is about to attack. For example, The first U.S. Olympic judo medalist ever, James Bregman, was a master counterattacker, especially against kouchi gari and ouchi gari. He seemed to always be able to anticipate the reaps and successfully counter them with swift foot sweeps. Another successful counterattacker, Peter Seisenbacher, had this same sense. Once, Seisenbacher was surprised with a kouchi gari, but he quickly countered with a painful juji gatame as he was falling to the mat. The opponent tapped out before Seisenbacher even touched the mat.

To develop this sense, you need a cooperative training partner. Your fellow judoka initiates attacks so that you can develop that anticipatory sense that lets you know an attack is imminent. One caveat: Counterattacks shouldn't be your primary source of scoring. Modern judo is highly aggressive in nature and waiting for opportunities to counter only opens you up to negative judo penalties.

In the photo sequences, note that *uke* initiates the attack and *tori* counters or finishes the throw.

Ouchi Gari Counter

1: Uke (left) positions his left leg behind the heel of his right foot. As he does this, he pulls tori's right arm forward and toward himself with his left arm. Uke's right arm is at shoulder height but also draws toward him. The position finds uke with the right side of his body facing tori.

2: Uke shoots his right foot between tori's feet in an effort to begin his clockwise reaping motion.

3: Anticipating the ouchi gari, tori sweeps both of uke's legs from behind. He does this the instant that uke begins his reap.

4: Continuing with his sweeping action, tori completes the counter because of the anatomical advantage.

Osoto Gari Counter

1: Uke (left) begins the attack with an *osoto gari*. He steps in with his left foot to the side of tori's right foot.

2: Next, uke kicks his right foot out and through his left supporting foot and tori's right foot.

3: Because tori is anticipating the attack, he should lean forward so uke doesn't have enough momentum. Uke's throw is stopped with his right leg hooked on tori's legs.

4: Tori now can swing his foot around far enough that he is leaning into uke, whose legs are still hooked from his initial osoto gari attempt.

5: Tori continues to lean into uke while keeping uke's legs hooked.

6: As tori kicks backward and upward with his leg, he lowers his head and drives his opponent to the ground with an osoto gari of his own.

Kouchi Gari Counter

1: Uke (right) takes the first step forward with the right foot because he wants to get in striking range to sweep tori's right foot and execute a *kouchi gari*.

2: Tori is anticipating this. He merely extends his foot as if to execute a *sasae tsurikomi ashi*. He does this as uke attempts to reap.

3: The counter sweeps uke before he knows what is happening. Notice how tori has pivoted his body clockwise while pulling hard and downward at the same time.

Uchimata Sukashi Counter

1: Uke (right) is getting ready to apply an *uchimata*, but tori senses his intention.

2: As uke is pulling and entering, tori draws in his left knee because he knows that his opponent must get between his legs in order for the uchimata to work.

3: Because tori had his knees together and swiveled to hide his hip, uke couldn't get his right leg in between tori's legs.

4: Tori now steps across and uses uke's momentum against him by twisting uke over with a *tai otoshi* on his standing leg.

5: Tori completes the counter.

Uchimata/Yokoguruma Counter

1: Tori (left) anticipates uke's attack.

2: Uke enters with an uchimata, but tori lowers his weight and encircles uke with his arms.

3-4: After stopping uke's momentum, tori shoots his right leg through uke's supporting legs. He torques and turns his body completely under and through. Because he is holding onto uke, uke is whirled over forcefully.

5: After smashing the mat, tori continues rolling until he is face down over his opponent.

Ushiro Goshi Counter

1: The *ushiro goshi* is a commonly used counter in judo and is usually executed on opponents who use a high-grip hip throw. Here, uke (right) begins to enter by stepping forward with his right foot. This should already alert tori, who should be anticipating how to counter the move.

2: As uke is drawing his left foot around to enter into a hip technique, tori has lowered his body. By bending at the knees, he makes it harder for uke to get his hip under tori. At the same time, tori encircles uke's waist with both arms.

3: With his hips still lower than uke's hips, tori begins to thrust his hips forward.

4: Continuing to thrust forward, tori eventually arches to the apex of the lift. At this point, uke's body should be tilted almost horizontally and the descent phase of the throw should occur.

5: Tori follows uke all the way to the mat to make sure that uke lands safely on his back for the score.

Te Guruma/Sukui Nage Counter

1: This counter is similarly executed in that tori's center of balance is lower than uke's. The only major difference is that tori's hand is placed between and grabs at the opponent's legs. Here, uke (right) is preparing to throw tori with a hip technique.

2: Tori lowers his hips by bending at the knees and maintaining his right-hand lapel grip. He releases his left-hand sleeve grip to place it in between uke's legs. He grasps uke's right leg.

3: While still maintaining his hold on uke, tori thrusts his hips forward and straightens his legs to lift uke off the ground.

4: To finish the throw, tori draws his left arm back, causing uke's body to spin counterclockwise to the mat.

5: As uke is falling to the mat, tori maintains his right-hand lapel grip. However, he does let go of his leg grip, allowing uke to be supported in his landing. Note: Official rules in 2010 state that this technique must be a counter and not an offensive move.

Tani Otoshi Counter

1: Uke (right) enters for a hip throw, but tori anticipates the attack.

2: When uke tries to sweep back with his right leg, tori lowers his hips by bending his knees. He simultaneously grabs around uke's waist with his left hand. Tori also shifts his weight over his left leg. At this point, uke's throw is effectively stopped.

3: Without a break in action, tori continues leaning to the left. He takes a quick half step behind uke's left leg and pulls uke off-balance to the left rear side.

4: Continuing to drop to the mat, tori's left foot may or may not come off the mat. However, it should be positioned such that it traps the opponent's foot from stepping back and possibly helping uke regain his balance.

5: On landing, tori should not be positioned underneath uke. To prevent this, tori draws his knee backward so that he will be looking at uke from the side. What is not pictured is that tori will turn in and face down to uke to finish the throw.

Tsubame-Gaeshi Counter

1: This counter is timing-dependent because it is a baiting maneuver. Here, uke (left) attempts a foot sweep. Tori anticipated the attack and sets up the trap to bait his opponent.

2: As uke sweeps, tori draws his left foot up, back and out of the way of the sweep.

3: Without skipping a beat, tori sweeps uke as soon as uke's foot passes by tori. In short, uke begins a sweep, but tori sweeps instead.

4: As uke falls, tori releases uke's right-hand collar grip so that uke can break his fall more easily. Note: Tori's foot never hits the mat. He just does a circular chase and sweep.

Feigned Combination Attacks

It is always a good idea to have a number of different combinations and feigned attacks in your arsenal to keep your opponent guessing as to what you'll do next.

Feigned combination attacks are two attacks done in quick succession. The idea is to overwhelm or get the opponent to overcompensate his effort to defend himself in one direction, then quickly use his off-balance defensive posture to hit him in a different direction. In the backward-and-forward track, the following combinations could work: ouchi fake to a tai otoshi, seoinage to osoto gari, or seoinage to kouchi gari. In the left-to-right or right-to-left track, the following combinations would be acceptable: *morote seoi* to a left ippon seoinage, right morote to a left sode tsurikomi goshi, left okuri ashi barai to a quick right okuri ashi barai, or a fake osoto to a quick-shift backward *kosoto gari*.

Ogoshi/Kosoto

1: Tori (right) readies himself for what looks to be a left-side *ogoshi* entry.

2: Uke senses an imminent attack and braces himself by pressing his right hip forward. This is a common defense to disrupt the proper distance tori "needs" for an effective entry.

3: What is not pictured is a quick forward/backward twitching action by tori's left-side hip and leg. He twitches forward, causing uke to do so, too. However, this is tori's feigned attack. When uke moves his right-side hip forward to defend against an ogoshi, tori twitches backward to get behind uke and drop him with a *kosoto*.

4: Follow-through is important and tori does not want to end up underneath uke after completing his throw. Note how tori is on his side while uke is on his back.

Osoto/Cuban Seoinage

1: Tori (left) holds on to uke's left collar.

2: Maintaining his grip with one hand, tori kicks his leg across as if to attack uke's right side. Note: Tori's body and leg appear to be going right, but his right foot never touches the mat to that side.

3: Tori quickly draws back his right foot and places it in front and just past uke's left foot. At the same moment, tori's left hand comes up from under uke's sleeve.

4: Tori uses his left hand to grip uke's left sleeve and right hand to maintain a grip on uke's left collar.

5: Now tori lifts uke's arm and quickly ducks under it while instantly dropping down to one knee.

6: Tori begins to rotate to his right side while pulling uke in even closer.

7: When uke loses his balance, tori continues to curl and roll his opponent over.

8: The throw is complete.

Right Morote Seoinage/Left Ippon Seoinage

1: Tori (left) readies to enter.

2: He attacks with a right *morote seoinage* by stepping across and down on the ball of his lead foot. However, he is careful not to step flat onto his whole foot.

3: He spins on the ball of his right foot to quickly change direction. Tori now goes clockwise, shooting his left foot and arm through.

4: Tori spins in place, grasping the opponent's shoulder with his left arm. Tori bends his knees and pulls uke forward and off-balance.

5: Continuing to pull forward, tori loads uke and straightens his knees for a throw.

6: What started out as a right-side throw finished on the left. Misdirected throws, like the one performed by tori in this sequence, often fool the opponent into defending in one direction when he should have been defending in another.

Right Morote/Left Sode Tsurikomi Goshi

1: Tori (left) has a natural right-hand grip on uke. He readies himself for entry.

2: Tori steps across as if to enter into a *morote seoinage*. However, tori is careful not to place his foot flat on the mat. He only makes contact with the ball of his foot.

3: Once he feels uke move to defend against the morote seoinage, tori quickly spins on the ball of his right foot and shoots his left foot clockwise and across the opponent. He also lifts uke's sleeve.

4: Once tori rotates into place, he bends his knees and off-balances his opponent. Uke should be stretched upward because his sleeve is raised high before tori pulls him forward.

5: To finish the throw, tori continues pulling uke forward. He straightens his legs.

6: Once uke is going over, tori releases the hold on uke's sleeve, allowing his opponent to break his fall correctly.

Right/Left Sasae Tsurikomi Ashi

1: This technique is done with two quick stomps. The first stomp is with the left foot in front of the opponent's right foot. Tori (right) is in a ready position.

2: With a quick motion, he places his weight on his left foot, leans back and raises his right leg as if to execute a foot technique to the right side.

3: Tori looks as if he is attacking to the right so uke leans in the opposite direction, hoping to avoid the attack. Tori, however, stomps down on his right foot instead of attacking with it.

4: Now having fooled uke and off-balanced him to the left, tori extends his foot to stop uke's foot. He pulls him over to the left side.

5: Tori completes the throw. Note: Remember the stomps should be a quick one, two and lean, and twist backward to a *sasae tsurikomi ashi* to the opposite foot.

Misdirectional Spinning Uchimata

1: Tori (front) is standing in front of uke in a right natural posture.

2: Tori steps across uke with his left foot. He places his weight only on the ball of his foot and by uke's left foot. At the same time, he pulls uke forward in a counter-clockwise position. Although not visible, tori's toes should be pointed toward uke in anticipation of a spinning motion in the opposite direction.

3: Spinning on the ball of his left foot, tori shoots his right leg between uke's body and his supporting leg. He places the back of his leg against the inside portion of uke's left leg.

4: With the opponent's leg caught, tori continues to spin counter-clockwise.

5: As he spins, tori lifts his leg and takes uke over.

6: Here, tori finishes the throw.

Ouchi/Tai Otoshi

1: Tori (left) is in a right natural posture.

2: Tori begins by stepping forward with his right foot.

3: His left foot catches up in preparation for an ouchi gari.

4: When tori hits the ouchi gari, he knocks uke's left leg backward. At this point, uke is leaning forward to compensate for the force of the backward-sending blow.

5: Having anticipated that uke would react accordingly, tori steps into position for a tai otoshi with his right foot first.

6: Next, he swings his left foot counterclockwise. Tori's arms prop up uke's body for the throw.

7: Finally, tori drops under and across uke. He uses his right leg to prevent uke's movements to counter.

8: Tori accomplishes the finish by extending his legs and pulling uke over.

Osoto Gari/Kosoto Gari

1: Tori (right) appears to be contemplating an osoto gari.

2: First, he positions himself for an osoto gari by stepping in with his left foot. He pulls uke's arms in close with his arms.

3: Next, tori steps through with his right leg and reaps uke's supporting right leg. In this instance, uke manages to block the throw. Rather than stop and move out, tori steps down with his right reaping foot.

4: Because tori has stepped down with his right foot, he is able to support his weight and can now use his left foot to sweep uke's feet from behind.

5: It's always nice to see the completion of a throw.

One-Handed Attacks

One-handed attacks are those techniques that can be initiated while only having one hand on the opponent. These throws are particularly effective against players who are slower and not used to one-handed judo. (See pages 37 and 47.) One-handed techniques can also be used to slow up a match where your opponent may be particularly quick and you may not want to engage him on his terms. The one caveat is that the technique should be done within a five-second span or you could incur a defensive shido. (This is a different penalty from a noncombativity penalty. A defensive shido is when the competitor overtly acts to defend him or herself, whereas a noncombativity penalty is given for not doing anything for 25 seconds.)

Here are a few special one-handed throws you may want to include in your family of techniques:

Ippon Seoinage

1: One of the more popular throws of judo is the ippon seoinage or one-arm shoulder throw. What makes this throw so popular is that it can be executed with one hand. When doing the ippon seoinage, you can grip hold of either sleeve or collar with one hand. Here, tori (right) grips the lapel.

2: He steps across with his left foot.

3: Tori brings his right foot clockwise for the second step. He also makes sure to pull the opponent forward. Note: The second foot needs to enter in far enough that tori is able to face the same direction as uke. Tori's knees should be slightly bent while he pulls uke forward to load him for the throw. Tori extends his knees.

4: Tori remembers to support the opponent's fall by holding on. He finishes his one-handed throw.

Soto Makikomi

1: Tori (right) is holding uke with one hand, although it is impossible to see from this angle. He also steps forward to draw uke toward him.

2: Tori draws his left leg counterclockwise and places his foot in front of uke's left foot. As he positions himself, he raises his arm high and across uke's face. At this point, both competitors should be facing in the same direction.

3: Tori steps across uke's right leg and pinches down with his arm on uke's. He begins to roll forward, turning to his left as if doing a front roll fall.

4: Tori completes the throw. Note: *Soto makikomi* is usually favored by heavyweights although middleweights and lightweights use this throw, too.

Sode Tsurikomi Goshi

1: The *sode tsurikomi* goshi is a quick way to get a point if the opponent is not prepared from the start. Here, tori (left) grips uke with his left hand.

2: Tori steps forward with his right foot.

3: He swings his leg around counterclockwise while raising uke's arm high in the air. Tori's knees are bent and his hips are in front of uke's body.

4: Tori pulls uke over his back by drawing the raised arm across his back. Once uke is off-balance, tori can even use his free hand to grasp the leg and stabilize the throw.

5: Tori doesn't attempt to grab his opponent's leg until uke is off-balance. To do otherwise would incur a penalty.

6: Tori can also assist the throw by raising his left arm and shoving uke's legs over. Here, the throw is complete.

De Ashi Barai

1: Tori (left) has drawn out uke by pulling on his opponent's right sleeve.

2: As uke is about to commit his weight to his forward foot, tori sweeps. The timing is crucial because if uke commits his weight, then tori won't be able to budge it.

3: Tori sweeps to the side and high while pulling down hard.

4: Tori finishes the throw. Note: The *de ashi barai* is done one-handed but you can also do it with two.

Okuri Ashi Barai

1: Tori (left) and uke move laterally in a rhythmic movement. Tori plans to execute an *okuri ashi barai*, which is similar to the one-handed de ashi barai.

2: Tori holds uke with only one hand. They continue moving sideways, toward the reader.

3: When uke's right foot moves toward his left, tori sweeps. The action is swift and powerful.

4: Tori sweeps both of uke's feet off the mat. Tori's left hand actually pushes uke's arm into uke's body. He pulls down hard once uke is airborne to complete the throw. Similar to the de ashi barai, the okuri ashi barai sweeps one foot into the other rather than in front of the other foot. This technique is usually executed while moving sideways in a rhythmic movement. As one foot is stepping towards the lead foot, Tori adds momentum by sweeping hard.

Multi-Grip Attacks

Multi-grip attacks are executed where the initial entry is with one grip. Then the attacker changes to another grip allowing for a better anatomical grip to finish the throw. For example, the French judo champion David Douillet would often enter holding a normal grip, then once in tight, would swing his arm lower to grab the belt to finish off with a throw. In fact, judoka Ryoko Tamura used a multi-grip attack to defeat her opponent Amarilis Savon at the 1997 World Championships. Tamura gripped high, which fooled Savon into taking an uchimata. Tamura then slid her hand down to a more advantageous position wherein she could throw Savon with a seoinage.

With the International Judo Federation 2010 rules change, leg grabs and direct pick-ups became illegal. This means that you can only grab a leg if you have already off-balanced the opponent with a technique first. (The same idea also applies to counterattacks wherein you can only grab the opponent's leg when the opponent's attack can be countered with a leg grab.) Therefore, you'll probably see more multi-grip attacks, like ouchi gari from a regular grip with a switch to a leg grab on the lifted leg or a kouchi gari first to a kata guruma second. The possibilities are numerous.

Instant Attacks

Instant attacks are one of the hardest types of techniques to master. Even the concept seems foreign to all but the most stellar judoka. As discussed in Chapter 3, the instant attack occurs when the judoka is gripping. It may be at the start of the contest or after a matte is called and a re-engagement is about to ensue. For the attacker this is a practiced move. He or she must have practiced the feel of gripping and attacking without hesitation. He or she has to feel the weak moment and strike swiftly. Think of the entry as a charge, only in the case of judo, the charge is a throw. Japanese lightweight champion Tadahiro Nomura would often catch his opponents with an instant sode tsurikomi-type throw on the re-grip. Likewise, Ryoko Tamura would instantly do an uchimata when grabbing her opponent's judogi. Toshihiko Koga from Japan also uses instant attacks—gripping, then instantly attacking with a seoinage.

Low-Risk Attacks

As discussed in Chapter 3, low-risk attacks are attacks that have a low probability of being countered, penalized or leaving an opening in which the opponent can counter when executed. Low-risk attacks can include various types of combinations—kouchi gari to leg pick, ouchi gari to leg pick, right osoto gari fake to a switch, back right kosoto gari, or drop seoinage to a turnaround morote gari.

What is advantageous about low-risk attacks is that they are not usually expected and therefore harder to counter. Since 2010, straight-on kata guruma and morote gari have been generally frowned on by officials because they look too much like modern wrestling moves rather than judo. However, the tactical competitor and coach may find them useful for a one-handed-grip tactic in which the competitor maintains distance without initially having to take a grip first, still complying with the 25-second penalty rule of stalling for time.

Other low-risk attacks are a feigned harai goshi or soto makikomi. In doing them, you get defensively pushed away and then intentionally fall to the outside or to the mat. Yes, this stops the match, but you are still credited with having applied a technique within the 25-second penalty rule. Otherwise, if you are proficient at mat work, continue to assert yourself on the ground. For drag-out time, your ground techniques must look as if they may succeed. If not, the referee will halt the action and penalize you. Tactics like this, as discussed in Chapter 3, are best done in the latter half of the match when you're ahead.

To learn how to effectively execute low-risk attacks, apply them with the cooperation of a partner. Gradually, the training partner should increase his or her resistance to the technique, until there is virtually a contest. How fast the training partner increases his or her resistance depends on the competitor's progress in learning the technique. Coaches should monitor that progress, too.

True/False

1. **There is no particular way or order needed in a family of techniques. Instead you just need to have a family of techniques.**

2. **The principle of primacy states that favorite techniques are the most important.**

3. **Low-risk attacks, combination attacks and one-handed attacks should be considered for your family of techniques.**

4. **Whatever you can think of, you can do even without practice.**

5. **Keeping a record of what you are doing is a waste of paper and ink.**

Answers: 1.f, 2.t, 3.t, 4.f, 5.f

Chapter Review

1. Briefly discuss what a family of techniques is and list at least two benefits.
2. Briefly discuss the process of grooming and its benefits.
3. Give an example of the law of primacy.
4. Explain why some techniques work better than others in combination.
5. Explain the benefits of low-risk attacks.
6. List how you would train your athlete in developing a family of techniques.

"*The general who wins the battle makes many calculations in his temple before the battle is fought. The general who loses makes but few calculations beforehand.*"

—Sun Tzu, author of *The Art of War*

Scouting Your Opponents

CHAPTER FIVE

Scouting Your Opponents

or the 1997 Paris Judo World Championships, Amarilis Savon of Cuba had been well-coached by one of the world's best judo instructors, Ronaldo Veitia. At the competition, Savon faced Ryoko Tamura of Japan who began the match with her characteristic and flashy moving style. Savon moved cautiously in response, attempting a foot sweep here or a hip technique there; she did just enough to avoid a noncombativity penalty while waiting to draw Tamura into a technique and counter. Savon managed to preempt each of Tamura's assaults. She particularly guarded herself against Tamura's left and right hand grip. In fact, Savon's coach had warned Tamura in practice that if she gripped high to watch out for an uchimata, harai goshi or osoto gari. If Tamura gripped low, Savon could expect a drop seoinage. Armed with this information, Savon appeared confident whereas Tamura looked uncertain, wildly looking for an opening.

Midway through the match, Tamura gets a high grip on the wily Savon. It seems as if Tamura is going to execute a high harai goshi, which Savon plans to counter. Savon steps forward when out of nowhere she is upended. The action takes the players to a distance of about three meters, causing the two judoka to look like a swirling ball from beginning to end. What happened? Tamura had executed a successful seoinage. Savon looked to her coach as if to ask: "How could that be?"

Unless you have a keen eye for details, you may not have noticed how Tamura's hand slid down from the high harai goshi grip to her seoinage hand position. It all happened in a split second with no time to warn Savon. A video replay would have also shown Tamura's sleight of hand. Again it would be too late to do anything about it, but the information would be invaluable for future reference. Any coach or competitor becoming aware of this could now make preparations for the next time. This is essentially what scouting is about—studying the opponent so that you know what to expect.

Competitive Profiling

While you can always just watch your opponent to see what key mistakes he or she makes, you might not always remember them. It may also be difficult to catch the finer points of the opponent's game. This could be especially challenging for coaches who need to recall everything that their athletes need to know.

The profiling method provided in this manual is one that can be used to better understand your opponent when he competes against other opponents. Also, coaches should want to do a competitor profile not only for the opponent but for the competitor, too, should the competitor match up with that opponent. The more you see your adversary in a competitive environment, the more you will get a feel of how you might fight and defeat him. Likewise, the more the coach will understand how to improve the competitor's strengths and vulnerabilities. It is best to see how the opponent and competitor do against various levels of judoka. This way you can look for trends, although this can

Queries

1. Why is scouting important?

2. What is one of the best ways to scout the opponent?

3. What equipment is needed?

4. What are we looking for?

5. What do we do with the information?

be a time-consuming processes. Coaches will probably only want to do this for their best students.

The competitor profile sheet provided in this book generally takes 45 minutes to an hour to complete for each five-minute match. (For more detail, see pages 166-167.) This is because you'll probably need to replay your video of certain parts of the match several times in order to understand what happened or didn't work. Of course, if you already have a written system, then feel free to stick with it. You may want to add or subtract the items as needed, but it's probably a good idea to do a complete profile several times before editing it down. Here's a list of the elements in the competitor profile:

Worksheets courtesy of Hayward Nishioka

1. **Evaluator:** It is important to know who the evaluator is. Some evaluators are better than others. Usually, coaches are better evaluators than athletes because coaches want to understand why a competitor or adversary won and lost; athletes tend to just know the outcome.

2. **Event:** Some events are more difficult than others. It would be nice to know whether it is a local tournament in which a competitor is testing out some new skill or a major event where there is little room for experimentation.

3. **Date:** Dates are important because two opponents may have met at the same event multiple times, and you want to see if there are any performance differences over time.

4. **Names of contestants:** Of course, it is always a good idea to know who is doing what to whom. If you are filing hard copies by alphabetical order, this information should be at the top and perhaps in capital letters.

5. **Representing:** Athletes change affiliations all the time. For example, American judoka Jimmy Pedro represented a foreign team for a while. It's important to know a judoka's affiliation because it will tip you off as to the training and resources that have been made available to him or her.

6. **Division:** Division changes are always occurring, and a judoka may perform differently from division to division. For example, let's say a judoka who regularly competes in the lightweight category gains weight. He decides that rather than diet and go back to his original division, he will go into the heavier division where he may face a more troublesome opponent.

7. **Round:** What round a competitor is winning or losing in may be important to know. If he is losing in the later rounds, it may be an indication of lack of conditioning or perhaps psychological stress.

8. **Stances and grips:** One consideration that should not be overlooked is whether the competitor is left or right dominant or alternates his stance. Some competitors will stand right but attack left. Grips should also be looked at carefully; note where and how a grip is taken. Although most grips do not have fancy Japanese names, they are nonetheless techniques or pre-techniques that lead to success. For this

If a *judoka* likes to bully and run down his opponent, then it may be a good thing to know.

reason, the sample competitor profile in this book has figures that allow you to quickly number down or circle areas where the competitor takes a grip. There is also space for commentary to jot down idiosyncrasies on how the competitor takes grips, if he or she changes grips and whether he or she is able to counter a grip.

9. **Techniques:** The traditional concept of judo was to develop a favorite technique. In today's competitive world, the technique that you happen to win with is your favorite technique just for that instant. Major competitors usually rely on about four or five techniques. If in your scouting you compile a list of these techniques, then you know what to expect and what to prepare for in training. If you are a coach listing your own competitor's techniques that she uses in a stress situation, then you know what you have to work with. For example, let's say your competitor has three techniques: left osoto gari, left ouchi gari and a left *kosoto gake*. What do you think you might recommend she develop for her next technique? (Answer: A technique that moves to the front should come to mind.)

10. **Grip time to attack:** Once in a great while you will see a three-second match. It starts with a bow and ends with a throw within three seconds. BAM! It's over. That's what happened to judoka Yoshio Nakamura from Japan in 1996. He made it to the Olympics but only lasted for three seconds of competition before his opponent, Stéphane Traineau of France, threw him. Because Traineau lost his next match, Nakamura wasn't even able to use the repechage system for a shot at the bronze medal. Now that's fast. Had the heavily-favored Nakamura known that Traineau attacked off the grip, he might have avoided being thrown and lasted longer at the Olympics. However, the Japanese team has never been known for profiling competitors. Don't make the same mistake!

11. **Attack by minute 1,2,3,4,5/Score:** Looking at the form, you will notice there are boxes under each minute and that there is a vertical line dividing each box. This is so that you can tell how closely the competitor is adhering to the 25-second attack rule. Better players are aware of this rule and make an effort to attack on the front half and latter half of the minute. To the side, you will notice there are scores that may be circled for a yuko (Y), wazari (W) and ippon (I) as well as what technique was used to score. What is interesting to note are the patterns that emerge from recording a number of matches of the same competitor or opponent. If the competitor is beating everyone in the first minute, then he's probably a good technician. If he's beating everyone in the last minute, then he's probably in great cardiovascular shape. You will be able to tell if he is a fast, slow or consistent starter; whether he knows how to maintain a lead or fizzles out and gets scored on; etc.

The white belt's coach, if filling out a competitor profile, might notice that his athlete is having difficulty gripping. The coach might conclude that the young judoka must work on gripping faster or wear a proper-fitting gi.

12. **Penalties in minute 1,2,3,4,5/Comments:** If trends appear in the kinds of penalties a judoka incurs, you can use this information to your advantage, too. For example, if in a number of preceding matches you find that the opponent has received a noncombativity penalty in the first minute of a number of matches, you can then plan to use low-risk attacks to cause the opponent to incur penalties. Another example of how to use this information is if you find that the competitor or opponent is getting a lot of penalties in the last two minutes. This may indicate a weakness in cardiovascular capacity. If it's your competitor, perhaps he needs to concentrate on cardiovascular capacity a bit more. If it is the opponent, you can make him work harder in the match by running him.

13. **Win, lose, time:** This is merely a quick way to look at who won and how. You should also document how long it took for the competitor to win.

14. **Grips, breaks, taking a grip, control, changes on grips:** As mentioned, gripping skills are essential for any major competitor. These skills can be separated into how well a competitor breaks a grip taken by the opponent and how well he can make or take his own grip on the opponent. Control means how well the competitor is able to neutralize the effects of the opponent's grips and hold dominance over the opponent. Changes on grips refers to how some competitors will change

their grips from right to left or high to regular. It also refers to applying a technique in order to gain an anatomical advantage; for example, changing to a high grip allows the competitor to execute an uchimata or harai goshi. Of course, quirky or unfamiliar gripping situations can arise, but once known, they are no longer a surprise.

15. *Transitions to the mat:* Generally, when competitors fall to the ground, they are in danger of incurring a penalty unless a technique is executed within five to 10 seconds of hitting the mat. These penalties can occur if the referee is unfamiliar with mat techniques or if the competitor experiences an initial defensive shock after hitting the mat. What you are looking for is the stellar competitor who

Knowing that your opponent has been thrown to the left-rear side in his three previous matches is something you should definitely note.

has prepared how to use this moment of indecision and shock to his advantage. In the popular *Judo Ippons* video series by Fighting Films, two-time Olympic gold medalist Peter Seisenbacher is knocked down with a kouchi gari, but as he is going down, he flips his leg over the opponent's extended arm. Before hitting the mat, Seisenbacher executes a juji gatame arm lock. If your competitor were to have a match against him, this would be a good piece of information to know.

16. *Mat work in 1,2,3,4,/Comments:* In this section, you'll pay attention to whether the opponent is capable of offensive or defensive mat work. If you see that he does not seem to do well on the ground, this gives you good insight as to how to approach the opponent in a competition. If, however, he aggressively works the ground, maybe you should look elsewhere for an advantage. Any interesting bits of information on groundwork should be noted here in the comment section.

17. *Tactics/Comments:* Refer to Chapter 3 to see some of the tactics you should keep an eye on while scouting.

18. *Observed weaknesses:* These are obvious problem areas for the competitor or the opponent, such as physical condition, strength, mat work, one-dimensional style—the competitor has one technique—weakness in gripping or tactics, etc. Whatever it may be, write it down.

19. *Plan of attack:* This section is where you will take all of the above information and synthesize a plan of attack for your athlete.

True/False

1. You can quickly find weaknesses with or without a video set-up.

2. How a competitor stands and grips can determine what he may use as a technique.

3. Attacks per minute may determine the discipline and condition the competitor is in.

4. Tactics are easy to spot and to record.

5. A plan of attack is one of the first things you consider.

Answers: 1.f, 2.t, 3.t, 4.f, 5.f

Equipment

If you have ever played football, basketball or baseball at a college level, you will have watched films or tapes of the game to review for areas of improvement. If your school is one of the major players in the sport, it probably also had access to video equipment with special options like freeze frame, slow motion, advance frame-by-frame, reverse frame-by-frame, etc. The equipment might even have had the ability to have lines drawn over the screen. The purpose of this videography was to isolate the strengths and weaknesses of the opposition. As such, a good judo coach or competitor should also study tapes and devise drills for himself or his athlete to overcome deficiencies seen on film.

Image reproduction and special effects are commonplace today. Still there are some caveats in your choices. The basic equipment is a video camera, a tripod and a computer. Should you want to step it up a bit, there are special-effects programs that can overlay images with lines, arrows or circles, do split images—the works. Let's start with camera formats.

Video cameras can be VHS, S-VHS, VHS-C, but that technology is dated. They will work just fine but like classic cars, parts are harder to find and not as easy to handle. Unless you have a VHS player, your better option is to go digital. Today's digital cameras have fewer moving parts and are very durable. Prices have also come down considerably. Two major digital formats exist. One uses a mini DVD, and the other uses either a digital disk or chip. Most likely the dominant format will be the SD chip. SD 8 GB chips are now readily available to consumers and afford the videographer at least 20 minutes of continuous shooting. Tapes will obviously last longer. Direct transfer XD chips are also available. The nice thing about XD chips is that images can easily be imported into your computer for storage or editing via FireWire or a printer.

Video cameras themselves are very powerful today. Many of them are able to pick up an image in low-light conditions as well as shoot and magnify distant images up to 30, 60, or 100 times larger. There is a downside to the magnification, however. The further away the subjects are, the shakier the images will appear. That is the nature of cameras. Moving images are also harder to track. In addition, even though video cameras are smaller and more portable today, it is harder to keep them steady, even with two hands and a nonshake feature. This is particularly true if you are going to use a handheld camera over an extended period of time.

That's why tripods are a must if you plan to take a lot of video footage. Unless you have a steady camera on a good tripod, you will have a difficult time studying your shaky videotapes.

When filming competitions, professional videographer Dennis Yonetani uses a high-end Sony DVD camera on a fluid-head tripod. He edits with the program Dartfish.

It is best to purchase a fluid-head tripod—one that allows you to pan, or move the camera from side to side, without any jerky movement from you or the tripod. For travel, you might look for a lightweight tripod that is durable and solid as you look through the viewfinder. Often times you will find that if your tripod is too light, it may move as you pan. If the head is cheap, it will shake as it resists the new direction. The fluid head should be easy to control and adjustable as well. Good tripods are out there, but they start at about a hundred dollars. You really need to take your camera with you and test out the feel and control of your camera on the tripod of your choice before you tape a tournament.

For shooting video for judo, purchase the best equipment you can afford. Your video images will be a reflection of your equipment's ability to take good images.

Equipment Tips

1. Check your camera the night before shooting video.

2. Check your battery to see if it is adequately charged.

3. White-balance your camera because color adjustments will be better set.

4. Scope out the best vantage point to shoot from. Close is good. Try not to have people or a distracting backlight obstruct your view.

5. Test your focus and adjust to the range needed.

6. Avoid using the telephoto feature if possible because the focal length has a tendency to make images shake more.

7. If possible, avoid using the wide-angle feature because images often come out too small to see important details.

8. If possible avoid handheld videography because you will have shaky images, especially when shooting over long periods of time.

9. Follow your contestants with the tightest shots possible, leaving just a little room around the edges in case any unexpected movements should occur and your subjects move out of the frame.

10. Pan your subjects slowly and avoid jerky movements.

11. If there is a key area you are looking for, like a grip or foot work, zoom in on it.

12. Practice adjusting the pan, tilt, and the zoom button smoothly.

13. Before shooting, make a quick test shot, play it back and see if the image, color, and clarity are good enough.

14. If you are taping abroad, make sure you have the proper plug converters to charge your battery.

15. For some venues, you may have to gain permission to record.

Chapter Review

1. List and discuss the two major areas in this chapter.

2. Discuss what type of video equipment you would use and why.

3. Describe why it is important to list attacks per minute.

4. List the different gripping skills you might report on and why.

5. Devise a plan of attack for an opponent that your competitor is having a particularly tough time with using the profile sheet provided in the chapter.

True/False

1. The best way to study the opposition is to actually watch him or her competing while taking notes.

2. The S-VHS or super VHS is the best format today.

3. Digital formats can be stored and edited on your computer.

4. Tripods are really an optional item but important in wide-angle shots where you do not have to be present.

5. Taking video for judo-competition scouting purposes today is a simple process of point and shoot.

Answers: 1.t, 2.t, 3.t, 4.t, 5.f

"You cannot do a kindness too soon because you never know how soon it will be too late."

—Ralph Waldo Emerson, American essayist and poet

Communicating With the Competitor

Communicating With the Competitor

One day two Zen monks were sitting by a pond and looking down at the fish that flitted back and forth. One monk said to his companion, "Look at those happy fish swimming back and forth."

"How do you know they are happy?" the fellow monk asked. To which the first monk replied, "How do you know what I know about fish?"

Queries

1. What modes of communication are available to the coach and the coach/competitor?

2. How should you communicate with your athlete?

3. When should you communicate a problem situation?

4. What about mat-side at tournaments?

The story illustrates a communication gap between the two monks. The first monk has gained wisdom in empathy while the second monk hasn't reached the same level as the first; the second monk has no reference point in experience. While communication gaps can occur in many forms, the story depicts one of the most difficult—when there is no common experience.

The judo competitor and coach share a similar experience because the coach has knowledge that the competitor does not. The coach must somehow communicate across the gap to the competitor and, likewise, the competitor must come to understand the knowledge the coach is trying to impart.

The coach gives his athlete a double high-five for a great job. This nonverbal action really communicates a lot to the competitor and is important reinforcement of his performance.

Also consider this: There is a natural progression from being a competitor to that of becoming a coach. In many instances, fellow competitors will fill in the otherwise empty coaching seat to support a teammate or younger competitor from their dojo at a match because the official coach is busy elsewhere or because there is a dearth of good judo coaches in general. If you find yourself in the position of a competitor/coach, it's important to understand what your athlete is going through, the rules of the game, the areas your judoka may be lacking in during the preparation phase, etc.

Of course, communication can take various forms, and there doesn't seem to be one method that will work for everyone. This chapter will offer suggestions as to the four settings in which a coach or competitor/coach might talk with his athlete—formal, private, casual and mat-side.

Lectures and Chalk-Talk Sessions

A formal communication setting that occurs in judo is a lecture or chalk-talk session where the coach and competitor or competitors gather together to learn. For any real progress to occur, there should be regular sessions in which the coach covers his program and exchanges ideas with the athletes to get to the next level. This in turn helps the competitor develop a mind-set that also encourages him to get to a new goal. Generally, the best time for coaches to hold a lecture is before or during a practice session.

Depending on the coach's familiarity and relationship with his athletes, he or she may be able to go into more detailed issues, such as calling attention to individual judoka. However, this can be perceived as threatening to the competitor on a personal level. So if you aren't sure, you would do just as well to make a general statement—"OK, team. In yesterday's tournament, I saw several of our players with their backs to the line. What did we say the better option was?" Confronting issues like that also helps athletes in the group who may have encountered the situation without realizing it and less experienced members who have never encountered it.

No matter whether it's before or after a practice or competition, in a group or alone, you should log your experiences and from that make your future plans.

Jimmy Pedro Sr. coaches Olympic silver-medalist Ronda Rousey.

In lecture sessions, it's probably a good idea to include video reviews because it's hard for the competitor to ignore the truth of the matter. Videos don't lie, and your athlete will have to learn to appreciate the criticism because it is your duty as a coach to point out the competitor's problem areas. However, the key to critiquing is caring. You should never be mean-spirited about it. It's a learning curve. Everyone is there to help.

Private Sessions

Private sessions are usually held because the information may be of an embarrassing or sensitive nature for the competitor. Generally, you should reserve private sessions for the moments that need immediate attention—like when a person's zipper is down and he is about to address an audience. It's usually best to address the problem head-on to help the competitor find a solution for the problem, and get on with life.

Here are a few lead-ins to a private session:

1. Sam, can you drop by my office after practice? (In the office) I'm concerned about_____. Here is why, _____. Now what can we do about it? (Wait for an answer)_____. Thank you.
2. Erin, may I speak to you for a moment? Hygiene is for the health and safety of everyone. You need to _____. What do you think? (Wait for an answer) _____. Thank you.
3. Leslie, can we step over to the side? It has recently been brought to my attention that _____. Is that correct? (Wait for an answer) _____. I just wanted you to know I was concerned.

The Two-to-One Method

One very famous coach with a tell-it-like-it-is mentality once said, "I haven't the time to baby these guys. If they can't understand that I'm trying to help them, they can always go and find another coach." Of course, coaching is a matter of style, timing and the need of the moment. But what if that doesn't work for your competitor? What if you're coaching younger children? In that case, you might want to try communicating with them in a more private setting with the two-to-one method.

— Coaching Kids —

When you are coaching smaller kids, it's a good idea to lower your height. Bend down or sit down before talking to them. A big adult standing over a tiny tot who has just lost a contest can be intimidating for the little judoka. Be in control of your voice, what you say and how you say it. Remember that a young judoka is at the beginning of a, hopefully, long road to becoming a champion. Like any coach, you want their journey to be filled with development, fun and rewards. In some respects, it is more difficult to coach children than adults, and your worth as a coach/instructor is tested to a greater extent with kids.

This method works very well with competitors who are defensive and have a difficult time taking criticism. First, begin your critique on a positive note. Every match has a bright spot in it because no matter what has gone wrong, the competitor probably has done something right in the match, somewhere. Start with that, and for every one thing you can say positively about the competitor's performance, you can follow up with two negatives.

It's usually best to limit your critiques to two negatives because you start losing the competitor's attention with three or four. For example, you can say, "I really like the way you were able to control the opponent's gripping." This is praise. Now, follow up with corrections: "But remember what we drilled last week. You have to attack once you've gotten your grip. Use your ouchi gari to tai otoshi combination next time."

Here are a few good two-to-one lead-ins:

1. You did a good job on_____. Now let's work on_____or _____.
2. Great job with_____, but if you really want to succeed, try_____.
3. I want to commend you on your_____. Do you think you could also_____?
4. You did well under highly adverse conditions, but can I make a couple of suggestions_____?

Informal Settings

Informal settings are places where some of the best information is passed on because the information doesn't come with a directive to study, know, and be tested on what is said. These chats can happen before or after practice in the locker room, while going out for pizza or burgers, at parties, while driving to a tournament, etc. For the coach, it should be a relaxed time in which to recount past experiences of seeing, meeting, or even competing against champions.

Informal settings are generally when a coach will impart some brief comments, observations, recommendations or corrections as to how a competitor can improve

True/False

1. **Chalk-talk sessions are common in judo.**

2. **Chalk-talk sessions always involve videos.**

3. **When giving a critique, always begin with what went wrong.**

4. **Private sessions are for private matters.**

5. **One of the best informal methods of instruction is the storytelling method.**

Answers: 1.t, 2.f, 3.f, 4.t, 5.t

his or her game. The coach may also offer praise, which can really boost the spirits of some judoka.

Informal settings are also an excellent time to just tell a story. "Tell me a story" is a request that comes from every child's lips before bedtime because everyone loves a good story. Judoka are no different.

Stories act as guideposts, if told correctly. Stories are powerful tools because they aren't commands. Often, judoka hear a coach say something like, "Do 25 throws!" or "Bow correctly!" However, a story can bring better results. Wouldn't you feel more driven to train if a coach said, "Do you want to learn the technique that helped Yasuhiro Yamashita win the 1984 Olympics?"

Here it is an example of storytelling in action:

"The first time I saw an ushiro goshi was when I was just 10 years old. I was sitting cross-legged on the mat, which you don't see as much anymore. The brown belt competitor tried a harai goshi on a white belt. They were both facing me, and if the brown belt had been successful, they would have landed on me. I don't know that I could have gotten out of the way in time. My legs were numb from being there so long cross-legged. I was lucky though because the white belt wrapped his arms around the brown belt and picked him up. As he arched to get some height, the brown belt's feet went past my face on the way up. On the way down, his body was a blur. What I do remember was the brown belt's body slamming onto the mat so hard that I bounced off the mat. One of my classmates asked, 'What technique was that?' My instructor said, 'That's an ushiro goshi.' And today, that is the technique I'm going to teach you all."

It's also important to note that the training programs for assistant instructors for the United States Judo Association and the United States Judo Federation require candidates to relate a personal experience of having seen a technique in action as part of their teaching demonstration because of how powerful a teaching tool it can be.

Tell a Story

Stories helped this author while he grew up and practiced in a *dojo* in East Los Angeles, and he uses memories from that time to inspire his students. Here is one:

Sen Shin Dojo was the brainchild of Ryusei Inouye. He built two duplexes on the side of a hill in Los Angeles. In the back, he created his American answer for the Kodokan—a four-car garage complete with a restroom and an anteroom. Instead of cars, he filled the garage with sawdust, packed it down and covered it with a canvas. On the west wall, he placed a small wooden shrine. This place became Sen Shin Dojo. After practice, he'd turned the lights out in the main makeshift dojo, but the seniors would sit around, drink beer and talk about everything under the sun, but mostly judo. Names of famous judoka like Shiro Saigo and Masahiko Kimura would come up. Often, they would reminisce about fantastic feats of throws done so hard and swiftly they would knock a person out. As Inouye-sensei and the senior students and instructors would talk, I would peer into the dark corners of the dojo and see these spirits moving, throwing, pinning, as if they were somehow alive again. I recall that one night we spoke of the qualities of champions, like hating to lose, fighting until you couldn't even stand up, trying when there is no hope of success, etc. Then, one of the senior black belts said in his heavy Asian accent, "Just like Hayward." I couldn't believe my ears. In the midst of all these great legends, he had referred to me. In an instant I was proud, embarrassed, overjoyed and humbled.

Now there's a story and an idea for you to use.

Mat-Side Communication

Mat-side is where you communicate with your player while he or she is competing in a tournament. Of course, some coaches advocate that trying to coach a player mat-side is a little too late and more of a distraction to the competitor. Others believe that mat-side communication is a good way to remind the athlete of things you two have worked on while in the heat of competition: "Get your grip

Photo by Pamela Yamane, Kaizen Concepts

Different coaches have different signals so that other coaches and competitors can't understand what they are trying to communicate to their competitor for the win.

first!" or "Keep your hands in front!" The thing to remember about mat-side communication is that it doesn't only tell your athlete what to do, it also lets the opponent know what your competitor is aiming to do.

While doing coaching with mat-side communication, you have to be careful not to antagonize the referee. You have to be tactful by not directly coaching the referee. Don't yell, "Noncombativity ref! Where's the penalty?!" Instead, say, "Good job, Kenny! You've got him on the run. Keep attacking because he's tiring. He doesn't have energy to attack." This tacitly reminds the referee that the opponent should get a noncombativity penalty while telling your competitor not to allow any attacks. However, it also lets the opponent know he needs to attack to avoid incurring a shido.

If the opponent can also hear you coaching your competitor to do his favorite technique, you need to get around that. Some coaches develop a numbering system that assigns certain numerals to certain techniques or certain tactics to certain letters. This takes some coordination, however, and to be successful, you should practice using the system in the dojo during practice. The competitor needs to get accustomed to hearing the command and knowing how to integrate it into his game. Of course, there are those players who zone out all voices and noises when competing. If your competitor is like that, then hopefully your constant and redundant promptings will be enough to carry the day to victory.

Another means of mat-side communication is through prearranged hand signals that only you and your competitor understand. Baseball is famous for using various secret signals between catchers, pitchers and coaches. Of course, if your competitor is constantly looking at you for direction, the signals may be too much of a distraction, especially in a fast-moving sport like judo. The signals should communicate all the competitor needs to know in a glance, usually in-between the "matte" and "hajime" commands. Then again, prearranged signals also need to be trained into the competitor during practice sessions at the dojo.

Redundancy

At the end of most kendo practice sessions, each *kenshi* (a kendo student) goes in front of each instructor and formally bows to thank the instructor. At this time the instructor will give advice to the kenshi as to how to improve. Many times it is the same advice given over and over by the various instructors. This is so that when the time and conditions are right, the kenshi will understand what he needs to do to improve. It's called redundancy, a process of repeating a correction over and over again. It works in judo as well. Show and tell a beginner how to tie his uniform belt correctly in a square knot enough times, and usually the student will learn to tie a square knot when he is ready to know how. The first time he may have been in too much shock to think about square knots. The second time he was probably more relaxed and focused enough to listen and learn.

One caveat: It's usually wiser not to tell your competitor to do a technique you have not first practiced with him in the dojo. It is counterproductive to tell your competitor to do a Koga seoinage because you think that technique will throw the opponent. Unless your guy has been working on one or is capable of doing one, you probably shouldn't be coaching him to do a certain technique or tactic on the spot. His lack of exposure to the technique may make the competitor vulnerable to counters. If the competitor does try the recommendation and loses, it's not fair for the coach to criticize the competitor's actions.

It is always difficult to stay objective during an emotional event such as a tournament in which your competitor is moving one way and you think he or she would be better moving in another way. This is especially true if you have invested

Caring is one of the most important ingredients to successful communication. It may be more important than what you know about the game.

valuable time in preparation. For the wiser coaches, they know judo is an ongoing process of knowing your competitor, knowing your opponents, knowing the rules and making corrections over a long period of time. It doesn't do to just comment at mat-side because then you just end up a cheerleader.

Communication Issues

Moods and conditions are also a factor in communication. It is usually difficult to communicate with your player if he or she is temperamental and has just lost a match. It might just be more prudent to wait until a later and more private time to talk to your competitor. If your player is adult enough to accept constructive criticism, then the best time to cover mistakes is right after the match. That way the match is still fresh in the mind of the competitor as to what happened and what needs to be done about it. How a competitor takes criticism has to do with how you approach a critique. While you as a coach may have to make your own sacrifices and have your own concerns, remember your intention and role is to improve his or her performance. Granted, judo hierarchy favors the coach, but to maintain order, a good coach knows how to act according to his or her athlete's attitude and ability and still get the teaching point across.

Chapter Review

1. Discuss the chalk-talk session and what it is for.
2. Explain the two-to-one method.
3. Give an example of the two-to-one method.
4. Describe a (brief) story about the best match you ever had.
5. List three benefits of mat-side coaching.

True/False

1. **Mat-side coaching can warn the opponent about what the competitor is planning.**

2. **You are not allowed to coach the referee directly.**

3. **Some players just can't hear you when they are competing.**

4. **Redundancy in critiquing is a good thing.**

5. **Don't criticize what you haven't coached your competitor to do.**

Answers: 1.T, 2.T, 3.T, 4.T, 5.T

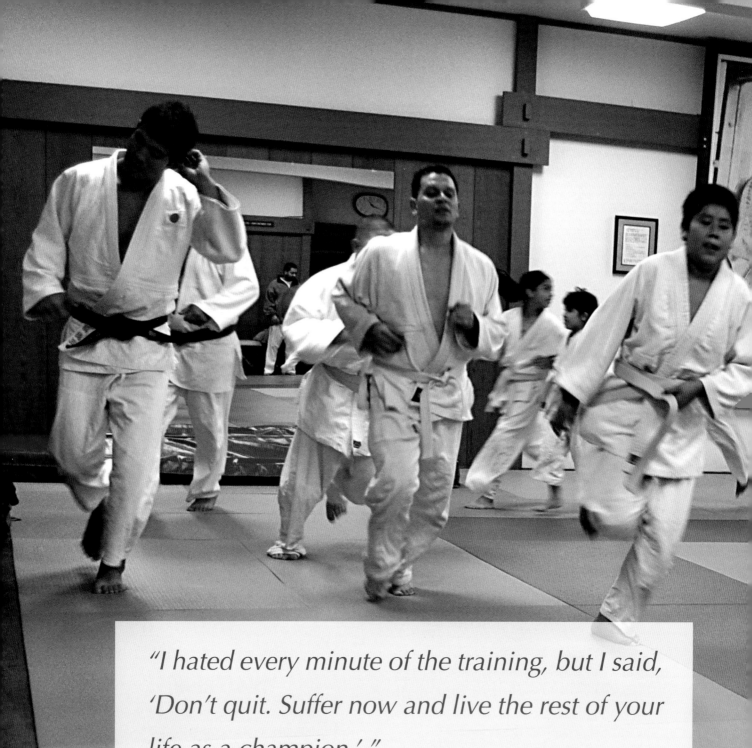

"I hated every minute of the training, but I said, 'Don't quit. Suffer now and live the rest of your life as a champion.' "

—Muhammad Ali, world heavyweight champion

Cardiovascular Conditioning

CHAPTER SEVEN
Cardiovascular Conditioning

In 17th century Japan, a lone samurai was walking on the Tokaido Road when three rough-looking men with drawn swords surrounded him.

"So, you're the samurai who is said to defeat his opponents with no sword, eh?" they asked. "Well, how about against three of us?"

Queries

1. With what physical attribute did this swordsman defeat his opponents?

2. What are some exercises that can get you into better condition?

3. How do you physiologically prepare for competition through aerobic vs. anaerobic exercise?

4. What changes in history produced the Olympic sport judo?

5. How does judo competition develop resilient and stronger athletes?

The lone samurai merely kicked his off his *geta* (wooden thongs) at two of the assailants and began to run away.

"Look," the ruffians shouted to one another as they began to chase the lone samurai. "The coward runs for his life."

Despite the pounding footfalls of his assailants, their taunting curses and the nearby swishes of their blades, the lone samurai managed to run just out of reach of their sharp weapons. In the distance, the samurai saw a town so he picked up his pace imperceptibly. While running, he turned his head and heard the panting of only two of the three assailants. After some time, the samurai reached the town's edge, stopped and calmly turned to face one tired ruffian. Only one had managed to keep up with the samurai, but now that assailant was in no condition to fight. In fact, the man was just trying to suck in enough air to stay upright.

The lone samurai suddenly screamed loudly at his attacker, who promptly fell to the floor in fear. Because of the difference in their physical conditions, the lone samurai was able to outrun and defeat the assailants without drawing his sword.

In *kenjutsu*, or the art of the sword, the ultimate victory is to win without having to draw your sword. Miyamoto Musashi, the lone samurai, proved he understood that lesson very well.

As illustrated by the ruffians in the story, one of the most neglected components of conditioning is that of cardiovascular readiness—the ability to sustain a quality attack pattern for the full duration of the match or matches. Perhaps this is due to the fact that it is more difficult to perceive and track cardio fitness. With the resistance component of training, you can see muscular growth. With the technical component, you can see a technique. With a tactical component, you can see the results of a tactical maneuver. However, the lungs, heart, vessels and uptake of oxygen at the muscle tissue level are a bit different. So, what would be a simple test of cardiovascular preparedness? In the official International Judo Federation rules, the competitor has to make a serious attack every 25 to 30 seconds or face a noncombativity penalty. Thus in a five-minute match, there should be a minimum of 10 attacks in which the offensive competitor attacks once every 30 seconds. This type of effort expends a lot of cardiovascular energy, especially if the opponent is in better cardiovascular condition, physically stronger, on the offensive, and has better gripping skills. Thus, participating in a cardiovascular program is a must for high-level athletes who want to be on the aggressive end, which is the winning one.

Evolution of Cardiovascular Conditioning

As discussed in Chapter 2, judo stems from jujutsu, a martial art intended to incapacitate or kill the opponent using an array of practiced techniques. Because of this goal and because the techniques could cause serious injury, historically, jujutsu practitioners practiced their skills in slow, methodical and prearranged movements called kata. The kata were designed to improve the ability of the practitioner's attack or defense without harming anyone in training. In-house dojo contests to determine the effectiveness of the training also helped as long as there were no serious injuries. Serious injuries not only cut down on the time the jujutsu practitioner could train but also weakened his fighting unit, should it belong to an army. In addition to all that, the jujutsu practitioners were tested immediately in the field as warriors, usually with little practice and disastrous results for the practitioner. In the end, this was the physical conditioning allotted to the ancient jujutsu practitioner, and the more time a practitioner had to practice, the better his chances were for survival in combat.

All of this changed with the advent of the modern era, the Meiji Restoration, Jigoro Kano and the rise of judo. The emphasis in the martial art switched from killing to athleticism and living more effectively through, as Kano called it, gamesmanship.

Today the goal of the judo athlete is to win in judo competition. This is accomplished through a well-planned training regimen designed to optimize performance in all areas necessary for the competitor to meet the demands of a particular event. You've learned about many of those components in previous chapters, but now it is time to consider the physiological and cardiovascular components in modern practice.

In the past, traditional judo relied heavily on the practice of *kata* and less on randori, uchikomi entry drills and nagekomi throwing drills in order to train the individual. The latter types of practices add greatly to the aerobic capacity of the individual while the former mainly aided in setting up nerve patterns, which are often referred to as *waza*. In the past, it was more important for the practitioner to practice kata because he didn't have a training partner to help him perfect his techniques. Today, science and the sportslike mentality of judo have shifted the emphasis from rote memorization to aerobic capability.

The success of judo over jujutsu schools in the mid-1880s is due to Jigoro Kano. Because of his exposure through international travel to Western sports and the Olympic movement, Kano gained insight into methods of practice that would increase skill level, an athlete's number of wins, general athletic performance and human experience. His method of practice removed the dangerous aspect in the martial arts and was termed randori or "free sparring." *Ran* in Japanese means "chaos," and

Seiryoku Zenyo

Kano had some interesting ideas that equated judo to how people live life. First, he said the body is the instrument for the purpose of life, without which you have nothing. He argued that people should use their bodies in the most efficient manner possible in order to live a more meaningful life. One of his maxims was "maximum efficiency with minimum effort" or *seiryoku zenyo*. Therefore, ingrained in the practice of judo is the desire to do things better with the least amount of energy possible and still get the best result. When you apply a judo technique, you don't apply brute force, you apply Newtonian principles. You pull the opponent off-balance, lower your center of gravity under the opponent's center of gravity, apply the principle of force—increase force on one arm and decrease the resistance on the other arm—use a little torque and voila! The opponent is upended. Kano further advised that these principles, as learned through the practice of judo in everyday life, would develop not only the body, but the person as a productive human being as well.

dori means "to grasp" or "to catch."

In randori, judoka move about the mat and try to find order while alternating between attacking and defending. The practice of attacking and defending randomly forces the participants to keep alert for unexpected attacks and opportunities to attack from all directions. This is different from kata because the movements aren't prearranged or expected between the practitioners. Moreover, randori practice places stress on the cardiovascular system, which helps the judoka build up a tolerance to fatigue. Less fatigue means fewer mistakes and more attempts at throws, pins, chokes and armbars. More attempts mean more improvement in all areas of training competition, and that leads the competitor to greater chances of winning. This was the difference between the old, kata-based practice of jujutsu and the fast-paced randori practice of judo: Judo practitioners were more aerobically trained to win.

In addition to randori practice, judoka now use ancillary methods of practice. These include calisthenics—sit-ups, pull-ups, push-ups—jogging and various ukemi, if partners are unavailable for a quick warm-up before doing randori.

Early judoka were hesitant to include such supplemental methods because elderly sensei believed that time spent lifting weights or running was time taken away from practicing judo. The real reason behind the hesitation was probably because many martial artists of the time weren't sure how to use ancillary methods or how to incorporate these methods to maximize competitor performance. It wasn't until the introduction of physical education during the Meiji Restoration that a formalized system of warm-up exercises, or *junbi,* appeared in Japan. Calisthenics came into play with the introduction of Western sports such as baseball, track and field, gymnastics, etc., to Japan. In fact, weight training didn't become *de rigueur* until Donn Draeger trained Olympian Isao Inokuma in the 1960s.

Today, judoka know that raising the body's core temperature before working out cuts down on the incidences of injuries and readies the individual for a more rigorous practice. They also know that additional practices may be used to enhance performance through isolation of certain muscles groups that normally could not be overloaded sufficiently. Thus, plyometrics, pilates, aerobics and weight training are utilized as training methods that can zero in on specific areas that need improvement.

True/False

1. Historically, those who have more training were more likely to survive in an actual battle.

2. The modernization of Japan was pivotal in adding a cardiovascular component to judo as well as changing its mentality to that of a sport.

3. The use of kata, *uchikomi* and randori aid in developing aerobic capacity.

4. Even in traditional Japanese martial arts, a system of calisthenics was used to warm-up the body to prevent injuries.

5. Judo has always employed a regimen of auxiliary training methods.

Answers: 1.T, 2.T, 3.T, 4.T, 5.F

Aerobic and Anaerobic Conditioning

Ancillary training methods are important tools that enhance a competitor's performance in competition. At the top of our list is the need for the judo athlete to be in peak cardiovascular condition in order to endure, at the least, the duration of one match. Ideally, the judoka trains so that the athlete doesn't run out of steam when the pressure is on, and one way to accomplish this is through aerobic and anaerobic conditioning.

Cells in the body prefer to get energy via oxygen. Thus, aerobic shape refers to a person's ability to process and provide air adequately so that the body has enough oxygen and does not become fatigued; the body metabolizes energy aerobically. When cells are forced to work in a state where they do not receive enough oxygen, the body switches from aerobic to anaerobic metabolism. Your aerobic and anaerobic abilities depend on your current level of fitness. Examples of aerobic activity include long-distance running, cycling, lap swimming, race walking or any activity that keeps the heart pumping for at least 20 minutes. In contrast, examples of anaerobic activity include 100-meter races, powerlifting and gymnastic events.

Judo requires aerobic conditioning to meet the demands of long randori training sessions, in which the competitor practices and hones different techniques. Judo also requires anaerobic conditioning to provide the short bursts of energy needed to apply throws and mat techniques. The competitive judoka uses both aerobic and anaerobic conditioning interchangeably and all the time when doing judo.

Judo requires the grace of a gymnast, the strength of a weightlifter, the conditioning of a runner, and the timing and heart of a gunslinger.

It is important to increase the anaerobic threshold to be able to execute more attacks per minute over a longer period of time. More attacks that are successful means the nerve impulses are not only increasing, but they are firing more efficiently. If they are firing more efficiently, the chances of throwing your opponent and winning are increased. So where do we start?

Various ancillary training methods try to raise the anaerobic threshold to mimic an aerobic condition. Obviously, the first evident result would be better performance with less fatigue. Physiologically, the body has changed. Studies in exercise physiology indicate that aerobic conditioning increases red blood cells, which are the cells that carry oxygen to the muscle tissue. The ability of the muscle cells to take up oxygen is also increased. Carbon dioxide and other waste products such as lactic acid are eliminated more efficiently. There is also an increase in the volume of blood pumped out with each beat, all of which, when put into a judoka, can result in a better physiological machine that is able to increase the number of attacks per minute, thus increasing the chances of the competitor winning. This also decreases fatigue and decreases the possibility of making mistakes. Physiological conditioning is a key factor in elite competition as well as a plus in just having a fun time in randori.

Target Heart Rate

Physiological conditioning has a lot to do with how fast your heart pumps blood throughout the body. The HMO Kaiser Permanente suggests the following formula for calculating your target heart rate, or THR, which is the rate you want your heart to beat during exercise:

Men	Women
220 – athlete's age x .65 = THR	225 – athlete's age x .65 = THR

The two numbers, 220 and 225, represent the upper limits of how many beats per minute your heart should be beating during a bout of exercise. To go beyond these numbers—220 for men and 225 heartbeats for women per minute—would be injurious to the heart. (Note: More recent studies indicate that the formula for women should be recalibrated to a more conservative rate of 206.)

Age is also a consideration in this cardiac exercise formula because no one would expect a

70-year-old to run a mile at the same pace and at the same heart rate as a 20-year-old. Therefore, you subtract the athlete in question's age from the maximum heart rate.

The .65 actually represents a percentage rate (65 percent) that measures how hard a person works during exercise. It is also a percentage that can be adjusted to meet your needs. For example, many Olympic athletes hoping to attain a high anaerobic threshold will work at a higher percentage, many times above 80 percent. So, to calculate what your THR should be when you work at 80 percent, you would multiply .8 with the result of the maximum heart rate minus your age. Thus, 75 percent would be considered a good in-between rate.

The result of this formula represents the target heart rate, which is the rate at which the heart should be pumping. In order to increase performance, your heart should pump at your THR for 20 to 30 minutes three to five times a week while exercising for at least a month.

Example THR Equations

220 (maximum heart rate) - 20 (young athlete's age) 200 x.75 (work rate) 150 The number of beats per minute during a bout of exercise for 20 to 30 minutes (THR)	220 (maximum heart rate) - 40 (young athlete's age) 180 x.75 (work rate) 135 The number of beats per minute during a bout of exercise for 20 to 30 minutes (THR)

Keeping in mind the 220/225 THR formula as a guideline, begin gradually pushing yourself. You might first try working at a 65 percent rate to see how you do. If you should find that your heart rate goes over your target heart rate, then back off. This means you aren't ready to perform at that level. If your rate does not come down to your resting heart rate after a few minutes of rest following a bout of exercise, consult a medical professional. On the other hand, should you feel relatively comfortable with your exercise regimen, it's time to step up to the next level. In order to progress, you need to work just beyond your comfort zone. As you are working, monitor your breathing and your ability to tolerate the level at which you are working. It is best to keep a logbook of your workouts to track your progress.

Overload Principle

Consider what Bob Bowman, Olympic swimmer Michael Phelps' coach, had to say about training his star athlete: "I like to train him to exhaustion, then I ask him to do a little bit more." If you do only what ordinary people do, you will be ordinary. It's the extra effort that puts you a cut above and makes you extraordinary. The overload principle requires a person to do more than what he or she is used to in order to make improvements on performance. Once one level of improved performance is achieved, added effort is needed to reach the next level and

True/False

1. The most important attribute for a judoka is aerobic capacity.

2. The THR for an elite athlete is 225 – age x .65.

3. Judo requires an increase in aerobic and anaerobic capacity.

4. The reason for being in aerobic shape is to increase your quality training time.

5. Competitors who are in good physical shape make fewer mistakes.

Answers: 1.f, 2.f, 3.t, 4.t, 5.t

then the next. The overload principle works with muscles, bones, blood and blood vessels, the heart, lungs and even the brain.

As a general rule, the amount of improvement diminishes as the competitor reaches his ultimate goal. It will seem as if the athlete has to increase time, resistance, repetitions and spirit to attain the slightest of gains when he reaches the top of his game. This point of diminishing returns can sometimes be frustrating, and the competitor has to understand that this is when ordinary players give up. It is at this point that the devil is in the details—what you do that your opponent is not doing is what makes the difference in winning and losing—and the competitor can make it to heaven or go to hell.

One thing for coaches to remember is that not everyone is a Michael Phelps in a judogi. Be judicious in how and whom you train. Somewhat like jumping into a Japanese hot bath, physiological/cardiovascular conditioning is about going in one toe at a time and taking your time as you learn your limitations.

Specificity of Exercises

When you want to build up your leg muscles, you don't do push-ups. Specificity of exercise requires that the exercise be closely related to the area you are trying to improve. Thus, you would do squats, knee extensions, leg curls or toe raises to strengthen the leg muscles. Additionally, if you try to improve cardiovascularly, you would work aerobically and not anaerobically. In contrast, weight training may be of some benefit aerobically but it may not be the most time-efficient way to improve cardiopulmonary capacity. Here are some specific training methods that will help you do what you have to do; you will probably want to monitor your THR for any method that you choose:

Photo by Hayward Nishioka

1. *Interval training:* Unlike jogging around a track at a moderate and even pace, interval training requires intermittent bouts of all-out dashing. This can be done in a park, open field or road but is best monitored on a track. On the track, the judoka sprints at the straightaways and jogs when going around curves. He or she should repeat this at least 12 times around, possibly before or after a few miles of jogging.

2. *Fartlek:* A type of training that middle- and long-distance runners do to improve their cardiovascular abilities. They alternate all-out sprints with jogging when they are tired. There is no set distance or time they run when they decide to switch to jogging. Instead, the switch is based on the individual's condition. The better your condition, the longer you can probably sprint. You jog until you feel as if you can sprint and then vice versa. Do fartlek training for at least 20 minutes, and you'll find that you get the best results on uneven terrain—a few hills, trees, obstacles and straight-aways should be fine.

3. *Tire drag:* Fashion a chest harness to which you can attach a rope. The rope should be approximately 10 feet long. At the far end of the rope, tie a discarded or used car tire. Now run while dragging it. The

There are numerous ways to get into cardiovascular condition, but one of the most popular ways always seems to involve some type of running.

pace at which you run may vary, but try to run for at least 10 minutes. That length of time is a little more than it takes to complete a match with a golden score and then some.

4. ***Charging the hill:*** Find a hill with a 10-percent grade or more that inclines for at least 33 yards. Now sprint up the incline, all out, at least five to 10 times. Try to press yourself and not rest between runs. Remember to monitor your THR at the same time. Try to get a feel for your breathing with each sprint up the hill. Are you tired? Are your lungs burning? How about your legs? Are you about to give up? What level of pain or tiredness do you feel? Monitor or have someone monitor the information for each dash up the hill. On tough hills, don't be surprised if on the seventh or 10th time, your mind isn't screaming RUN. Instead, your body will only respond in slow motion.

5. ***Pull/push the car:*** Find an empty level-ground parking lot and select a clear runway. It's usually best to do this late at night after stores have closed and there is no traffic. You will need about 30 to 50 feet of runway. Have a friend stay in the car to steer and to stop it if needed. Tie a rope to the bumper joints long enough so that you will have a handle to grab hold of with both hands. Now start pulling the car across the parking lot. Your pulls should find your arms bending at the elbow as if to off-balance your opponent. If the rope is long enough, you can also mimic an entry into a throw such as seoinage. Once you have reached the opposite side, push the car back to where it came from. Repeat this seven to 10 times, resting as little as possible. Again, monitor your heart rate. After a month of practicing this regimen three times a week, you should notice a marked difference when practicing with opponents. Your body should be able to tolerate and surpass previous workload limits. If someone were to keep a record of attacks-per-minute during your randori sessions, you should show more attempts with less fatigue factor.

Photos by Hayward Nishioka

1: A great way to get into shape is to pull a car across a parking lot with judo-type arm movements. That means pumping and bending the elbows and rotating your body from right to left and left to right.

2: Without stopping for a break, push the car back and start again.

6. ***Obstacle course:*** Immediately when you think of an obstacle course, you think of a military one—high-stepping through tires, swinging over a mud pond, climbing over a high wall and crawling under barbed wire while bullets are flying overhead. Actually, any distance with any obstacle will suffice. The course doesn't have to be fancy. For the purposes of preparing for higher-level judo competition, an obstacle course should be designed keeping in mind the demands placed on the athlete during his or her match time. Included in the course should

be gripping, dodging, pulling, working in a bent position, quick lateral and circular movements, something on the ground, and an array of physically challenging movements. It would be nice to have a course designed for 10 minutes' duration, which is about the time allotted for a match, overtime plus a little extra. If constructed correctly, an obstacle course can be fun, challenging and very beneficial.

7. **Timed uchikomi:** Uchikomi drills are used to improve the ability to perform a technique. The idea is to have enough electrochemical impulses travel over nerve cells to excite the development and growth of new surrounding nerve cells, thereby bolstering signals to the muscle tissue to contract in a specified manner. Of course, correctness of form

Uchikomi drills not only aid in developing technique but may also develop your anaerobic threshold, if done with a degree of sustained intensity for the proper period of time.

is primary to the idea of speedy entries. It's a waste of energy to enter incorrectly and fail. It is better to set up patterns of muscular contractions to sequentially fire correctly first, then work on the speed of entry. Now, let's say we can execute 35 seoinage correctly in one minute. To accelerate to 45 entries per minute (p/m) and still maintain a level of excellence would stress the cardiopulmonary system. Which is exactly what we want. Now try to reduce the number of entries p/m and increase the minutes, first to three, four and eventually to five. Once you feel comfortable doing uchikomi for five minutes, increase the number of entries p/m till you are somewhere in your THR range. Rest till your heart rate comes down and then repeat four or five times.

8. **10 x 20 Nagekomi:** Nagekomi by themselves are just throws. You select a throw and throw a willing partner who takes the fall for you. Usually, nagekomi are done at a fair pace and, unlike uchikomi, you get to feel the full range of motion of the throw. For this to aid you aerobically or anaerobically, you need to increase the intensity level. So, do 20 nagekomi per person as fast as you can and do it with 10 partners or 10 times with one partner, alternating 20 times a piece. You will find some throws are more draining than others. It's best to select techniques you plan to use. Rest a bit till your heart rate comes down and repeat the drill at least four to five times. You will find that halfway through this drill, at about 100 throws, you'll have to really concentrate to do the techniques. Your partner will also find it difficult because he will need

True/False

1. **Auxiliary exercises are best designed when the principles of overload and specificity are included.**

2. **Interval training can be done anywhere as long as there are intervals of lowered heart rates.**

3. **Randori sessions can be aerobic in nature as long as your heart rate is constantly at or above your THR for least 20 minutes.**

4. **The better a competitor gets, the less progress the competitor may seem to make.**

5. **All of the auxiliary exercises mentioned are designed to increase only the aerobic capacity of the judoka.**

Answers: 1.t, 2.t, 3.t, 4.t, 5.f

to constantly get up after each throw to be thrown again. Thus, you may want to switch roles when your throwing technique begins to deteriorate.

Randori Sessions

Randori sessions serve two purposes. They are devised to stress the cardiovascular system and to train the nervous system to respond to judo movement under stress. In most recreational settings, practitioners will select a partner, practice for three to 10 minutes, stop, rest a while and, depending on their abilities and conditioning, repeat the process maybe four to five times in an evening workout. More often than not, the intensity level for randori is relaxed and recreational, and the rest periods vary.

In a competitive setting, randori sessions will also work to stress the anaerobic threshold. Competitors do this by having 10 five-minute practice sessions wherein they do not rest except for changing partners. During these sessions, the competitors' objective, of course, is to throw the opponent or at least attack every 30 seconds. Five minutes is the increment of time used so that the judoka will hopefully learn how long a five-minute match can last. Thus, randori sessions help competitors fine-tune their internal clocks to become aware of how much time they have to attack or defend in a match. The better athlete will keep tabs on her game during practice, and at the end of the five minutes, she will know by how much she has won or lost. In schools or dojo in which there are a few major players, they are placed in front the rest of the class, and the other judoka alternate in while the tougher players constantly stay in front and in the game.

Photo by Eric Nishioka

Randori sessions can be cardiovascularly taxing, especially if there are few pauses between tough practice partners. Of course, development of good techniques is primary here, but aerobic conditioning is a close second.

The other method is that of six eight-minute sessions. This is useful for competitors because they learn to sense how long a golden-score match would last. More often than not, the contestant who is not prepared physiologically or psychologically for a continuation of the match will give up. Six eight-minute sessions not only give the participants confidence that they can last the eight minutes, they also aid in improving cardiovascular endurance. Remember, it's usually in overtime that the less-conditioned athlete is saying to himself, "Damn, another three minutes."

In contrast, the conditioned judoka is saying, "OK, now you're mine!"

The five- and eight-minute sessions can also be interspersed or alternated but the usual time of practice is around 50 to 60 minutes in randori time. Again, the nice part of this cardiovascular-improving exercise is that you're improving your judo skills at the same time.

Chapter Review

1. List training regimen differences between ancient martial arts and modern judo.

2. List and discuss two leaders of judo and their impact on training regimens for modern judo.

3. List at least five benefits of aerobic training for judo.

4. Your athlete is your same gender and 23 years old. What is his or her THR?

5. List and discuss five methods of exercise that can improve your aerobic/anaerobic capacity.

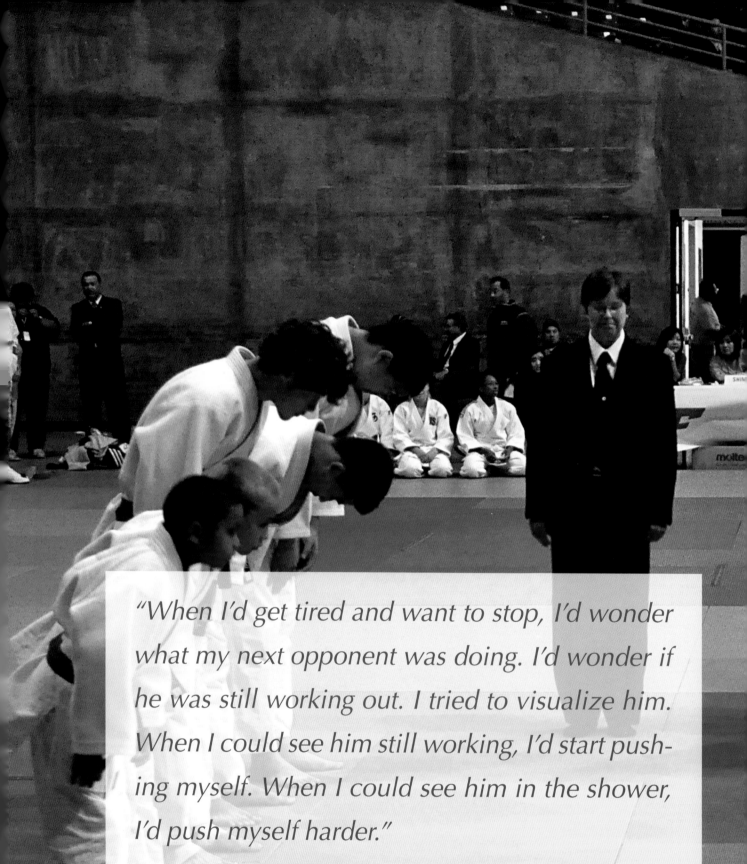

"When I'd get tired and want to stop, I'd wonder what my next opponent was doing. I'd wonder if he was still working out. I tried to visualize him. When I could see him still working, I'd start pushing myself. When I could see him in the shower, I'd push myself harder."

—Dan Gable, two-time Olympic medalist for freestyle wrestling

Resistance Training

CHAPTER EIGHT

Resistance Training

Kim, a *shodan*, was a light middleweight working out with a recent newcomer, Frank, who had first seen judo from the weight-training room at the local YMCA and thought he would give it a try. Frank, who was fairly new to randori practice, moved about gingerly because he did not know what he should be doing against a black belt. Kim sensed his hesitation and slammed into the 5-foot-10-inch, 220-pound weightlifter. He wanted to make sure that he could establish dominance over Frank early on before Frank became a more skilled judo player. Frank didn't know what hit him as he was lifted over Kim's left shoulder and unceremoniously dumped on the hard mat.

Wow, Frank thought. What was that all about? I can't let that skinny runt do that to me again.

When Kim gripped Frank again, he could feel the new judoka's tightened muscles instantly. This let Kim know that he was facing an opponent with a different attitude. Kim strained to look composed but he actually felt confused because he knew he wouldn't be able to get past Frank's iron-bar arms to execute his favorite throw, and he was right because Frank blocked his attempt.

The two came to a stalemate. Frank had enough strength and mass to defend against Kim's attempts to throw him, despite Kim's judo experience. Of course, Frank would eventually lose with noncombativity penalties in a tournament, but this was randori practice. The real vulnerability was the dent to Kim's confidence—he had thrown other beginners with ease, but Frank was a different story.

For one thing, Frank was not just bigger. He was stronger. His years of weight training and bodybuilding had turned him into an athlete. Frank was well aware of his strength and size and he knew he was a cut above the normal guy on the street. He had also developed an ego—one that would not permit him to just roll over and play dead at the first sign of adversity. The muscles he had built up had changed him physically and mentally and allowed him to do more than the next guy. In the end, Frank's strength was an equalizing force to the lighter, faster and more skilled Kim. Had Kim been equally as strong, the outcome might have been different. Had Frank not had the equalizing strength, Kim would most likely not have had a problem. And what if Frank had had the technical capabilities? Then the tables would have most likely tilted in his favor. The message here: Muscles make a difference.

Queries

1. **How do muscles work?**

2. **How do the nervous, muscular and skeletal systems articulate or interact with each other?**

3. **What muscles do judoka need to develop?**

4. **What do you need to do to develop the right muscles?**

5. **How can you track your progress?**

Muscles and How They Work

There are basically three types of muscles in the human body. The first type are smooth muscles, which are just that—smooth in appearance when viewed under a microscope. Examples of smooth muscles include the intestines, the liver, and the kidneys. Skeletal muscles are striated and connect to bones like your biceps. Striated muscles have bands of tissue packed tightly next to each other and are made up of actin and myosin filaments. When enervated, these filaments ratchet past each other, causing the muscle to contract. The third type of muscle is known as the cardiac muscle and falls within the skeletal group, but it is highly specialized in that it will still contract and expand when cut away from the body. In judo, you are mostly concerned with striated muscles because these muscles are responsible for moving the skeleton, which is how competitors get into positions to throw opponents and enact techniques.

If you have ever taken apart a piece of rope, you will find that it is made up of many strands of strings. Muscles are similarly made up of smaller and smaller parts that end in actin and myosin filaments. These filaments contract by sliding over each other. When they are contracted, they bunch up, shorten, and usually draw bones together.

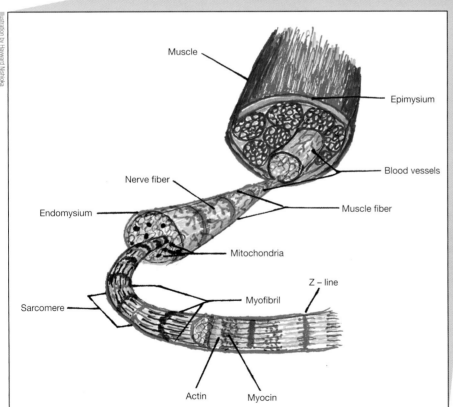

The basic makeup a of skeletal muscle includes filaments that lay close to one another and ratchet or slide against each other in opposite directions to shorten or contract the length of the filaments. As the names implies, slow-twitch muscle fibers contract more slowly than fast-twitch muscle fibers. Slow-twitch muscles can continue to twitch or contract at a steady rate for a longer period of time than fast-twitch muscles. This means that if you are genetically inclined to have more slow-twitch red-muscle fiber, then you're more aerobically able. You have a better chance at being successful in activities like long-distance running, Tour-de-France cycling or swimming the English Channel. Genetically speaking, you're gifted in processing air over a long period of time. Fast-twitch muscle fiber contracts at a higher rate and produces more power than slow-twitch muscle fiber. People with more fast-twitch muscle fibers are generally very quick and able to be explosive but only for short distances. They are good at 100-meter sprints, quick draws, sumo, long jumping, etc. There are also people who have a little of both. Those who gravitate to judo seem to have both types.

Science has found that people are just born one way or the other—some have more fast-twitch muscle fiber while others have more slow-twitch muscle fiber. However, that doesn't mean you can't train in sports that don't favor your genetic inclination. Your muscle type doesn't change; rather you just work to extend the limits of the one that you weren't naturally born with. A set of muscle fibers was recently discovered in the middle of fast- and slow-twitch muscle fibers that can be developed in either direction, according to Jeffrey Stout, Ph.D, an exercise physiologist at Oklahoma University. So, while you may think these scientific findings say that people are born to be sprinters or marathon runners but not both, the truth is much more complex. Yes, some people are born to be basketball players or racehorse jockeys, but anyone can also succeed despite the physical limitations or because of desire, hard work, expert coaching, the right environment, financial backing, etc. Who knows what can or can't be done? Whatever your physical makeup in judo, anyone can become a champion. It just takes work.

When you do weightlifting, you aren't creating extra muscle fibers. Instead, lifting results in the increased size of individual filaments; they enlarge rather than multiply. People are born with just so many strands of muscle fibers, and that's it. However, anyone can make these fibers bigger, and bigger is better because muscle size is related to the amount of energy a muscle can expend. Bigger muscles can expend more energy in pounds per-square-inch or psi. This really helps the judoka because the competitor with more psi—all other things being equal—has an advantage when it comes to all the pushing and pulling in a match.

Muscles are ensheathed with an outer layer of connective tissue known as the epimysium. Within the walls of the epimysium are blood vessels and nerve cells or motor neurons. The blood vessels supply oxygen and nutrients to the muscle tissue while the nerve cells send messages to the muscles by way of specialized nerve endings that attach to the muscle surface. These neural endings are called motor end plates. Recruitment and increased development of motor end plates results through sustained stimulation and utilization of muscle groups. In increasing motor end plates, you facilitate the sending of stronger messages to the muscles, thus allowing for the fine-tuning of motor movements. So, what should you take from all this? Enlarge your muscle fibers for added strength and fine-tune them to do specific movements, like a throw, through repeated resistance or weightlifting movements that mimic the technique's action to increase nerve patterns and motor end plates. (Think of uchikomi.)

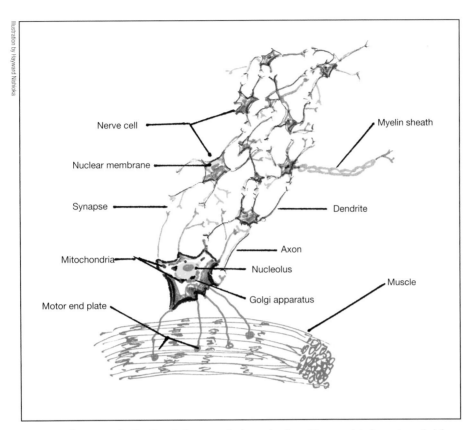

Nerve cell
Nuclear membrane
Synapse
Mitochondria
Motor end plate
Myelin sheath
Dendrite
Axon
Nucleolus
Golgi apparatus
Muscle

Nerves are the communication lines between our brains and actions. They consist of a center called the nucleolus and have arms that extend out to send and receive messages. These arms are called axons and dendrites. Millions of nerves are found throughout the body, but the strange thing is, they don't connect. Instead, there is a space between axons and dendrites that is referred to as a synapse. Over these gaps flow neural transmitter chemicals that terminate on the skeletal muscles by way of the motor end plates. On the other end of the pathway is the brain, which sends out the orders.

The muscles responsible for movement in a specific direction are termed prime movers. An example of a prime mover is the biceps brachii. It is the primary muscle you use to execute a curl; other muscle groups nearby stabilize or assist the prime mover and are referred to as assistors. Prime movers and assistor muscles may also be termed agonistic muscles. Agonistic muscles are often symmetrically opposed to antagonistic muscles. For example, the rectus abdominis or stomach muscles are symmetrically opposed to the erector spinatus or back muscles. Likewise, the biceps are symmetrically opposed to the triceps on the arm.

There are various types of contractions that occur in the muscle groups responsible for movement. They are:

1. *Concentric contraction:* The concentric contraction occurs when the muscle is shortening and pulling against the bones. It usually tightens the angle, such as when curling weights with the bicep from the thigh to the chest.
2. *Eccentric contraction:* The eccentric contraction elongates the muscle. Using the example of the bicep curl, this contraction occurs when you slowly lower weight back down to your thighs. There is still tension in the muscle, but rather than shortening the fibers, they are elongated.

3. *Isometric contraction:* In an isometric contraction, the muscle does contract but the bones don't move. There is still agonistic and antagonistic tension between muscle groups, too. An example of an isometric contraction is when you try to push something over. Your muscles contract to give you the force needed to push the object over, however the joints and bones in your hands and arms don't really move. Some researchers report that this type of contraction can help certain muscle groups generate a lot of explosive power at that angle of contraction. The concept is similar to what sumo wrestlers do when they practice their open-hand thrusts against a big immovable wooden pillar, which is devised precisely for that purpose.

4. *Isotonic contraction:* Isotonic contractions are regular contractions wherein the bones move through space as a result of a contraction. The angles may tighten or widen depending on the type of contraction.

5. *Isokinetic contraction:* An isokinetic contraction is one in which the resistance of the lift is pretty much the same throughout the range of motion. This does not occur in most lifting exercises because the pull of gravity against muscles can vary. For example, slowly lift a 10-pound weight overhead with your arm completely straight. Is it easier to hold when the weight is at the bottom by your thigh or when it is completely overhead? The easiest holding position is probably at the bottom of the lift followed by the top and lastly at 90 degrees when the weight is straight out in front. Gravity has played a different role in your resistance training at each of these angles. In an isokinetic contraction, all three angles would produce the same amount of resistance throughout the range of motion. This is usually possible with the aid of hydraulic, pneumatic or other specially designed weight machines that are connected to a computer.

6. *Plyometric contraction:* The last contractions are plyometric contractions, which are a kind of double contraction used by many elite athletes to improve explosive power. For example, say you jump down from a box. You contract the muscles to land safely on the floor, but then you immediately re-contract the leg muscles to jump up to another box. This is actually a drill used to gain leg power; the action is repeated for maximum training effect. The same double-contraction formula may also be used to develop other muscle groups. A medicine ball toss contracts the muscles of the arms, shoulders and upper torso when initially catching the heavy object whereas throwing the ball back immediately contracts them all again. Basically, you are causing one contraction after another in quick succession.

While all of this jargon seems academic, it is the language of resistance training, and an understanding of these terms and concepts will help you understand your body better and maximize your training effort. Now you can understand that muscles exert more force when they are bigger or have more psi. You don't get any more muscle than what you are born with; instead, you can just enlarge what you've got with "overload." When overloaded from different angles—concentrically, ec-

True/False

1. Muscles work by contracting, shortening or widening the angle of the bones.

2. Motor end plates can multiply and enervate muscle fibers to contract.

3. Prime movers are the muscles that are responsible for movement in a specific direction.

4. Isometric contractions mean that the bones move.

5. The principle of overload says that one needs to work on specific movements to develop judo-type skills.

Answers: 1.T, 2.T, 3.T, 4.F, 5.F

centrically, or even isometrically—the prime movers tire out but are "assisted." Muscles can create movement in a specific manner. If overloaded in a way that will affect that specific manner, motor end plates develop muscle fibers, causing specialized contractions, as in techniques, to occur. These specialized movements require concentric contractions of the agonistic muscles and a certain amount of relaxation of antagonistic muscles. To increase power for a given set of muscles, such as when lifting your opponents with an ogoshi, you can use plyometric exercises to contract your muscles explosively. You can also do isometric exercises to contract for a power gain at a certain angle, such as when resisting an armbar.

General-Strength Practices

General strength means the toning of all parts of the body. The most common way is to work out different quadrants of the body: upper front torso, upper back, lower front side, lower buttocks and legs. A popular practice is to alternate quadrants each day. For example, if you work out the upper back, work on another quadrant the following day. In resting, you give the soreness and lactic acid that builds up in the worked-out muscle tissue time to dissipate.

General strength is a requirement for elite judoka. Up until the 1960s, judoka devoted very little time to gaining extra strength through a weight-training program. All of that changed when an American named Donn Draeger helped train the legendary Isao Inokuma. Donn Draeger authored several books on the martial arts, but at heart, he was a judoka. One book in particular is *Weight Training for Championship Judo* (1966). It was revolutionary at the time, but weight training in today's highly competitive judo world is a must-do for elite judoka.

Weightlifting workouts should be preceded by warm-up and stretching exercises. Research by a number of exercise physiologists suggests that raising the core temperature of the body before any type of workout significantly reduces the chance of injury and also enhances performance. If you are just returning after a long hiatus, it is best to start out slowly with less resistance, intensity and repetition. For the older crowd, scheduling a physical check-up before getting back into physical situations may be the prudent thing to do.

There are several ways to approach the acquisition of general strength. Here are a few:

1. ***Sets and reps:*** As a general rule, weight training is done by sets and reps. Reps refer to the repetitions for a given exercise. Sets refer to the number of groups of reps. Thus, 10 reps of bench presses with a 100-pound weight is equal to one set. Normally, an individual does three sets of 10 reps. The reps may be increased or decreased depending on the amount of weight. To determine what amount of weight you should be working with, you should barely be able to lift the weight on the 10th repetition of the third set. For example, you're lifting about 50 pounds, doing 10 repetitions three times with a rest in between sets. Naturally, there is a bit of guesswork and experimentation at the beginning of your training until your baseline amount—the amount you can barely lift after three sets of 10 reps—is established. However, as you keep training, the amount of weight you can lift will begin to increase along with your strength.

2. ***Circuit training:*** This is yet another method used to generally strengthen the body. Ideally, it is done at a gym that is uncrowded but an area can be set up at home as well. At home, you may position a bench in a corner to designate station 1 and a jump rope at another corner to

designate station 2. Continue designating stations to finish your circuit—push-ups at station 3, a set of home weights at station 4, etc. Decide on the amount, time and intensity level you want at each station, then go from station to station and do those exercises at their designated locations. At some gyms, there may be an automated machine or a voice over a loud speaker calling out to members when to begin, stop and move to the next machine, mostly because of the higher ratio of participants to the exercise machines available. The obvious advantage of the circuit is that you can work all parts of your body during one exercise session. If done quickly enough and at a nonstop pace, circuit training may even result in an aerobic effect when you do the activity at your THR for 20 or more minutes. You'll train with weights and also get some aerobic conditioning in for the same price!

3. **"Burn, baby, burn":** This is another method of weight training, especially if you're adventurous or into the idea of "no pain, no gain." In this method, you pump iron till it burns. That means you disregard the standard sets-and-reps model and just do as many as it takes until there is a burning sensation in your muscles. The sensation will eventually cause you to slow down and eventually to stop. In this type of resistance training, your exercise will be shorter in duration if you raise the intensity or resistance level of the weight. When that happens, rest, do another exercise in possibly a different quadrant, then come back and do the same drill until it burns again. Usually, your second set will have a lower count of reps. The third will be dramatically lower. Thus, doing three sets should suffice but some training competitors may do more or less depending on the amount of resistance they're using. The toughest part of this drill occurs the next day when the muscle group you burned is in low-grade discomfort or even pain. This is because waste materials, commonly known as lactic-acid buildup, are still inside the muscle tissue. If you're planning to work out the next day in spite of the pain, it is advisable to warm up slowly and with lots of stretching exercises.

Having a Spotter

It is always a good practice to have a buddy when working with heavy weights because there is a possibility of having problems that require assistance.

There are those who relish the feeling of lactic acid, knowing that they worked hard and that the muscles are stronger for it, albeit a little painful. This is the difference between a recreational player and an athlete training to become a champion—no pain, no gain. In these types of extreme weight-training sessions, it's always wise to have a spotter. A spotter is someone who is there to assist you with the weights in the unlikely event that you overexert yourself and can't lift the weight anymore. The spotter may be a friend, a personal trainer or a coach.

4. *Pyramiding:* With this method, you start out with lighter weights as if warming up, then set by set, increase the weights until you are at your maximum lifting weight. If properly practiced, the lifter should be somewhat fatigued by this point. He then does sets with reduced weight. When

put in a graph, the exercise should resemble a pyramid because it starts light, ascends to its maximum output, then descends back down. In some respects, this kind of exercising follows the natural progression for many people who weight train.

5. **Lifting heavy vs. lifting light:** This is another method used when weight training. If you are interested in developing bulk, power and anaerobic capacity, it is better to lift heavy weights even if it means lowering your rep count. Instead of doing 10 reps, you may do only five or even as little as three or two on your last set. If you are looking for definition in your muscles or endurance-type strength, you may want to use lighter weights and do more repetitions. Doing 20 to 30 reps with lighter weights also has a tendency to favor the aerobic rather than the anaerobic model. But to truly be aerobic, the bout of exercise has to last at least 20 minutes.

Intensity

Whether you are working with light or heavy weights, the intensity level can have an effect on your weight training. Most people do not think so much in terms of the speed at which exercise is done, but if you're looking to improve muscular endurance, try going through your training regimen at half or less than half the regular speed. You may even want to consider slow motion. You will be amazed at how much harder it is to go slow than at regular speed. It also helps you focus on details of certain movements and muscle contractions. For example, slow curls mimic the type of action needed to resist a juji gatame armbar.

This is not to discount intensifying your exercise by speeding up. Speeding up your exercise necessitates quick contractions. These contractions are the kind you use in randori sessions in which semi-contracted muscles have to be fully and quickly contracted in order to enter into a technique and before your opponent has a chance to resist. Of course, if you're doing your sets correctly while weightlifting, the last set is going to be significantly slower than the first set because of fatigue.

6. **Saturation:** This type of general-strength practice can increase the efficiency of your workout. That is to say, if you had a workout in which you did 10 exercises and devoted an hour to completing them but allowed a two-minute rest period between exercises for casually adjusting weights, speaking to friends or just resting, you would have used up 20 minutes of your 60-minute workout time. That's one third of your time. In saturation workouts, the time between the 10 exercises is shortened. In fact, for some exercise-to-exercise intervals, saturation breaks are so short that your routine can almost turn into an aerobic activity. Usually this type of program of rushing through reps and sets is done with lighter weights and early in your planning season. Heavier weights can be used but, when considering the shortened recovery rate, they really are incompatible. It is conceivable that light weights and

True/False

1. **General strength can be developed through circuit training.**

2. **Pyramiding is when you start your exercise with the most amount of weight possible then work down in a pyramid.**

3. **Repetitive lifting of light resistance will yield the same result as lifting the same amount of heavy resistance in less time.**

4. **Saturation workouts are less demanding than normal workouts.**

5. **Exercise intensity, resistance, time and angle are factors in resistance training.**

Answers: 1.T, 2.F, 3.F, 4.F, 5.T

heavy weights can be selectively interspersed in your circuit to achieve saturation. The whole idea of this type of work is to saturate every minute of your 60-minute workout. You won't make many friends, but you'll get strong quickly.

Prescriptive Weight Training

Prescriptive weight training differs from general strength-building programs. Prescriptive weight training isolates areas of deficiency in the athlete and uses weight-training concepts and machines to erase the deficiency. While judo movement involves a coordinated and collective effort on the part of your muscles, the goal of prescriptive weight training is to strengthen and sometimes hyperstrengthen a deficient area. To best understand prescriptive weight training, let's look at the following situation:

John was having a particularly difficult time with Hal. Hal had a high grip behind John's neck and was bending John over just slightly. Two hands instinctively shot up to Hal's high grip in an effort to peel it off. Hal's left hand responded by gripping John's right sleeve in mid-effort. Hal pulled down John's sleeve toward the left side of his body. John tried to pull his arm back to his own side, but no matter how hard he tried, he couldn't do it. John not only felt uncomfortable, he felt vulnerable to Hal's right osoto gari.

The situation looked grim for John, and his arms were beginning to feel heavy and tired. In this position, he thought there was no way he could block an attack much less mount an offensive. He thought: Should I just drop to the mat and take a penalty? No. Maybe I'll attempt a throw and fall to the outside, then we can start anew. Why can't I get my arm back?

But oops! It was too late. Hal had taken advantage of John's weakened position and slipped in with his osoto gari for an ippon.

What went wrong in this situation? How did Hal get the advantage? Why couldn't John regain his composure?

One possibility for John's demise might be that he did not have enough general upper body and back strength. When Hal took the high grip to pull John forward, it gave Hal a slight advantage because it pulled John forward and extended his arm. In this position, John actually extended his arms further in his effort to peel away from the high grip. Hal had anticipated that and caught John's sleeve and pulled to Hal's side. This is when John's problems became evident. He didn't have the muscle power to reverse Hal's pulling action.

Situations like these usually happen in just a few seconds. Many times, a competitor will say, "As soon as I took a grip, I could sense I was in trouble." Or, if you're on the other side, you could be saying, "As soon as I took a grip, I knew I was the dominant one." When a grip is taken, it's a language all its own. It tells you about your opponent's left and right dominance, if he has fluid movements, how quick he is, and how strong he is. If you cannot respond correctly, you lose, and in this exchange, John could not respond with enough strength. If he'd had more strength, he may have had a better chance. How can John fix his problem?

First, the prime movers that control the ability of the body to maintain an upright posture are the rectus abdominis to the front and the erector spinatus to

Photo by Eric Nishioka

Coaches, should you find that your athlete is constantly having his arm pulled forward beyond the midpoint, you might prescribe a slow dose of pulling exercises. These exercises should draw the arm back in the opposite direction of the opponent's pull. Arms that are away from the body are usually in an anatomically weaker position.

the back. Because John's body was pulled forward, he needed to right his posture with the muscles on his back side. For his match with Hal, his arm and shoulder girdle weren't strong enough either so John needs to improve both areas.

Had John been weight training and developed better neck, back and arm muscles he might have neutralized Hal's osoto gari. Instead, John can do prescriptive weight training and use exercises like reverse sit-ups and bow-arching to strengthen those particular muscles. There are also exercise machines designed to accomplish these actions. There are simpler methods, too. For example, have a friend sit on your calves and hamstrings while the upper part of your body hangs over the bench, ledge or bed. Interlace your fingers and place them behind your head for support. Dip toward the floor, then rise up to a fully arched position. Repeat this as many times as you may require, although three sets of 20 reps is usually the standard and can be a challenge. You can also increase resistance by holding light weights or even extending your arms upward during the exercise. Plyometrically, you could have a second friend stand by your head and give you a swift push downward on the shoulder when you reach the apex of the reverse sit-up. If your objective, however, is muscular endurance, have your friend exert a constant pressure against your shoulders as you go through the sit-up's range of motion.

Of the two areas—his back and front torso and the arms with the shoulder girdle—the second area of concern is more complex. For one thing it raises the question of whether we should concentrate and train specifically for the problem of the left arm being pulled forward or consider symmetry and train on both the left and right sides of the body. On the one hand, if you weight train just the left-side arm, it may get stronger, perhaps even enlarge and get the job done in less time, but it could also end up lop-sided and cosmetically unappealing. It may even cause imbalance in subtle body movements. Whatever path you choose, the muscle groups that come into play are located in the arms, shoulder, and back muscles and the rotator cuff muscles, which include the supraspinatus, infraspinatus, teres minor and the subscapularis muscles.

Any pulling-type exercise such as the rowing machine, rope climb, or the pulling machines found in any weight-training facility will do. Often in dojo you may find tire inner-tubes wrapped around poles or bars or even nailed to a wall. These are usually used to pull against, to simulate a resisting opponent.

As you can see, prescriptive weight training only deals with the part of the body that is causing a deficiency. The hardest part of prescriptive weight training is learning how to correctly assess the problem. Once you pinpoint the problem, you only train those concerned muscles to overcome a resistance. For example, in the beginning of the chapter, you learned about Frank and Kim. If Kim had identified a deficiency in his arms and the back upper-torso muscles, he would have had a better chance at possible replays of his first throw.

Note: When doing prescriptive weight training, it is assumed that you will also have a general strength program going on concurrently.

True/False

1. **Prescriptive weight training is more specific in nature and deals with isolated deficiencies.**

2. **One failing of prescriptive weight training is that of symmetry.**

3. **Circuit training can be used as a part of prescriptive weight training.**

4. **In prescriptive weight training, you only concentrate on one muscle at a time.**

5. **Isometric contractions are utilized to maximize power at a specific angle.**

Answers: 1.t, 2.t, 3.t, 4.f, 5.t

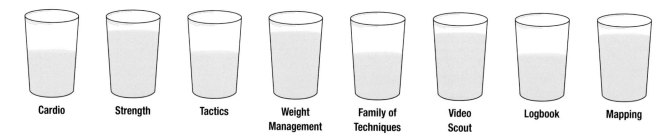

| Cardio | Strength | Tactics | Weight Management | Family of Techniques | Video Scout | Logbook | Mapping |

In modern competitive judo, weight training is just one of the glasses that needs to be filled if you hope to win. Crucial movements in a match can last for a second and are often easy to miss. One answer might be to use a video camera and/or a slow motion/stop action machine to look for key factors. For more about scouting, refer to Chapter 5.

Isotonic/Isometric Bands

The isotonic/isometric bands are just two bands, one is elastic while the other is not. The elastic inner tube or surgical tubing band gives you isotonic resistance to the point where the non-elastic judo belt gives you an isometric contraction. Isotonic contractions at the angle of contraction give you added power.

Earlier, you learned that when isometric contractions occur they can yield a lot of power. To better understand this, look at the following example:

After a competition, you watch your videotape and see that you are having a difficult time pulling your arm back from your opponent at a certain position. Because you understand isometric resistance, you know you need to create isometric resistance at that very position in order to complete your pull.

You can train for this using an isotonic/isometric band tied around a poll. An isotonic/isometric band is made of two bands—one elastic inner band that can be stretched to the second outer band or belt that halts the action allowed by the elastic band.

Repetitive pulls that go from an isotonic to an isometric contraction may yield the extra power you need to get your arm back to where you no longer feel threatened by an opponent. This kind of repetitive isotonic/isometric drill or uchikomi can yield great results.

Examples of Judo-Specific Exercises

In this section, there are examples that should give you an idea of the types of exercises and machines that can be used to strengthen deficient areas. Of course, you will usually have to observe videotapes to really spot deficiencies. The more seasoned veterans may be able to diagnose a problem quickly and prescribe a remedy. For example, John's coach might say to him, "You see how Hal keeps pulling your head down? I need you to work on doing reverse sit-ups and neck exercises. Do four or five sets of pulley exercises on the left side, too. You can't keep letting Hal draw your left hand forward beyond the midpoint between you and him."

General Strength Machines: Lower Body

The leg press machine will work many of the leg areas at the same time.

General Strength Machines: Upper Body

A pulley machine is excellent for shoulder-girdle strength. This pulley machine can be adjusted to suit various needs.

For the front upper body, this incline bench press will work wonders for your chest.

General Strength Machines: Free Weights

Don't forget the versatility of free weights. Here, the judoka is doing what looks to be a left and right seoinage entry drill with weight.

In the exercises that follow, you should be thinking, What muscles do I need to develop to improve my performance? Look at the exercises. Picture the movement and discover what it can do for you!

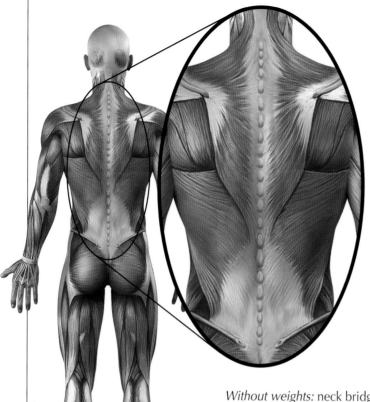

1. *Neck, splenius capitis, levator scapulae, sternocleidomastoid, upper trapezius, erector spinae:*

The neck and back muscles are essential in maintaining upright posture. High grips that pull down the head can be prevented with a strong neck. In ne waza, a strong neck allows for bridging out of pins and avoiding chokes. There are machines for the neck muscles, which usually work the neck in an up-and-down motion with the resistance trying to pull the head forward and downward. This tends to be one of the weak points of most recreational players.

Without weights: neck bridges, help from a buddy, self-contractions
With weights: neck machine, neck headgear

Prescriptive weight training focuses on mainly strengthening the areas of weakness. In this example, resistance training the muscles along the neck and spinal column would allow for a more upright and offensive posture. A bent-over posture denotes a defensive attitude and not only causes premature exhaustion—it's more difficult to breath when fighting to get upright—but also subjects the person to more penalties.

Photo by Eric Nishioka

2. *Shoulder girdle/rotator cuff, trapezius, deltoids, rhomboids, latissimus dorsi, teres major, pectoralis major, infraspinatus, supraspinatus, teres minor and the subscapularis:*

This set of muscles serves a number of functions. Besides stabilizing the whole shoulder area, these muscles aid in pulling, raising and pushing. What could be more important in judo?

Without weights: handstand push-ups, push-ups, chair dips
With weights: bench press, military press, incline press, shoulder rolls

Downward Pull

1: Beginning with the right foot forward, the judoka is about to begin pulling with his left hand. The left hand usually is the one that does the pulling to off-balance or pull the opponent in judo. (Note: He can adjust the pulley's height upward or downward.)

2: The judoka pulls and torques counterclockwise quickly but smoothly until he can turn no further. Notice his pulling elbow is raised and his head is turned away, which simulates the off-balancing pull of a throw.

3: The amount of weight used should be heavy enough that when you pull the weight, you will barely be able to complete a set of 10 repetitions.

Upward Pull

1: For judo, the upward pull is perhaps more important than the previous downward pull.

2: As he pulls, the judoka's elbow will be raised high. The motion will be a quick pull upward as if he is pulling an opponent forward and onto his toes for a throw.

3: As with the downward pull, his body is torqued to its furthest point before he returns to his original position. He uses enough weights so that he barely completes 10 repetitions. Also on each of the return phases, the weights should not be lowered completely between each set.

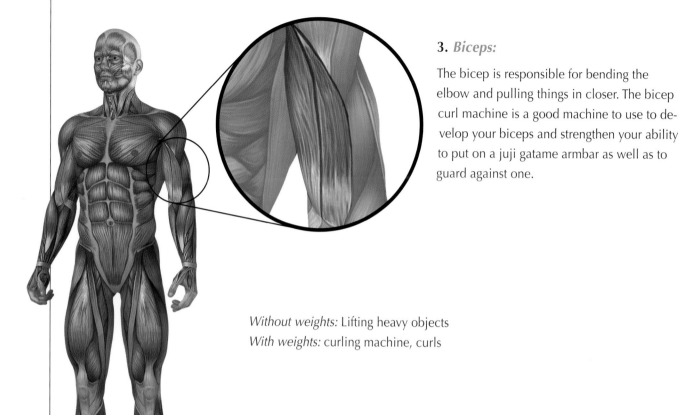

3. *Biceps:*

The bicep is responsible for bending the elbow and pulling things in closer. The bicep curl machine is a good machine to use to develop your biceps and strengthen your ability to put on a juji gatame armbar as well as to guard against one.

Without weights: Lifting heavy objects
With weights: curling machine, curls

Bicep Curls

1: The judoka begins with his arms fully extended.

2: Next, he pulls the resistance toward himself. This can be done quickly, much like he would do to pull an opponent in toward him quickly. Or it can be done slowly with heavier weights to simulate the taking of an armbar.

3: On the eccentric contraction, which is the downward extension of the arm, the judoka can vary the speed. If he goes as slowly as possible, it simulates an armbar, but as if you were defending against it.

4: As he reaches the end of his extension, he doesn't let the weight completely down but maintains tension throughout his set of 10 repetitions. He also maintains the usual breathing pattern for resistance training, which is to breathe in on the concentric contraction and breathe out on the eccentric contraction.

4. *Triceps:*

The triceps allow the arms to extend and to push things away. This is an important attribute because it allows you to defend against an opponent trying to enter into a technique. If you should view your videotapes and see that your opponent is getting in, part of the reason may be that your arms are not strong enough to keep the opponent out. That's usually when you need to work on the triceps.

Without weights: chair dips, push-ups
With weights: arm extenders, bench presses

Triceps Bench Press

1: Here the judoka does a triceps-strengthening exercise. Any bench-press type machine or resistance that resists the extension of the arms usually will develop the triceps.

2: While the judoka can do the usual set of 10 reps, he may also want to vary the resistance and go for more weights. To simulate his opponent getting in closer but being shoved away, the judoka can use poundage in which he can barely do a set of five repetitions of extensions.

Bench Dips

1-2: Bench dips can also develop the triceps. For extra resistance, the judoka can place weights or a heavy object on his lap while doing a set or two.

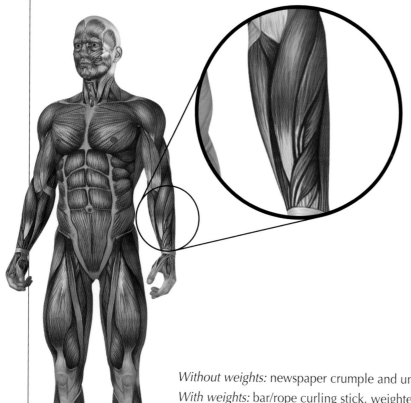

5. *Forearm muscles flexor profundus digitorum, flexor longus pollicis, extensor muscles, supinator longus:*

These muscles cause the hand to grip as well as flex ventrally, dorsally, laterally, and circularly. To the surprise of many, these muscles are largely found in the forearms. To strengthen one's grip and to fine-tune pulling and pushing skills, a good grip is necessary. There are many competitors who come off the mat and complain that their forearms are cramping up and they can't maintain a good grip. Perhaps a few resistance training exercises are in order to correct this deficiency.

Without weights: newspaper crumple and uncrumple, self-curl
With weights: bar/rope curling stick, weighted wrist curls

Grip Strengtheners

Photos by Hayward Nishioka

1: Using a peg, tie a rope with a weight to it. The weight should hang down about a yard and a two- to five-pound weight should be tied on the end. Extend the arms.

2: Begin to roll the rope and weight up. Once rolled up, reverse the process, but keep the arms straight and extended. Try doing this even beyond when your arms are burning.

3: Should you not have access to a device to develop your forearms, try crumpling and uncrumpling a newspaper page.

6. *Upper back:*

This contains the same muscles as the shoulder girdle. While these muscles are on the back side, they have more to do with the movement of the arms and shoulders. These are important muscles for the judoka since they have much to do with off-balancing opponents and pulling them in for a throw, pin, choke or armbar.

Without weights: rowing, reclined pull-ups, self-resistive pulls, door pulls,
With weights: universal machine pulleys, rowing machine, car pulling

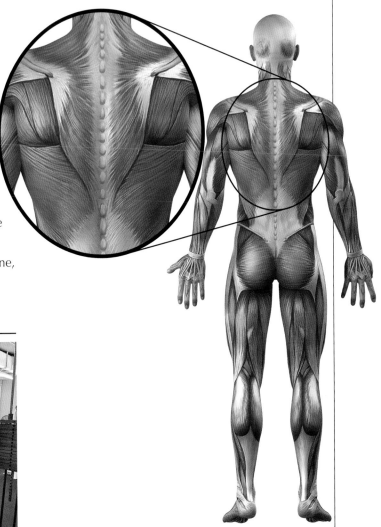

Lat Pulls

1-2: Another very good exercise for the upper back and arm muscles is the lat pull. This exercise works the latissimus dorsi muscle in particular, but it also will work muscles in the shoulder girdle like the infraspinatus, teres major and teres minor.

Rowing Machine

1: In the extended position, the judoka begins to pull by using the body and arms.

2: As his body begins to lean backward, his arms should begin to pull in until the handle meets his chest.

3: Once the handle of the machine cannot be pulled further, the judoka tries to "pinch" his shoulder blades. This is a very slight movement, but in judo, every millimeter counts. The action actually maximizes the contraction of the rhomboids.

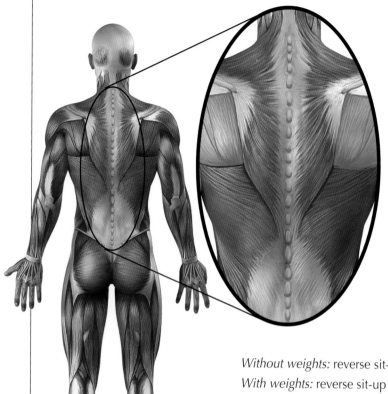

7. *Lower back erector spinae, lower trapezius, latissimus dorsi, internal oblique:*

The back muscles in conjunction with the stomach muscles aid in sustaining our erect posture. They allow us to arch our backs as well. Many of the muscles also allow for the beginning movements used in pulling, be it weight or person. For the judoka, the back muscles allow a more erect posture when your opponent is trying to bend you forward and off-balance.

Without weights: reverse sit-up, hanging-over-the-edge reverse sit-ups
With weights: reverse sit-up machine

Reverse Sit-Ups

Photos by Howard Nishioka

1: One of the easiest methods of strengthening the back is with reverse sit-ups. These sit-ups are not as easy as they may look because they use fewer muscles than regular sit-ups. The judoka begins with his hands behind his head.

2: From the ground up, he begins to arch up until he is almost completely arched. He repeats the action as many times as is necessary until he can't do any more. As with any exercise, he writes down how many he did, then tries to improve on that number as he progresses.

3-4: Another option for this exercise is to do the reverse sit-ups with weights. You may want to use more weights and do fewer reps. You may also want to do them snappier as if you were quickly pulling an opponent forward.

8. *Upper torso front:*

This contains the chest muscles that are used to push objects away from us, but they are also important in the process of breathing. The pectoralis major and the anterior deltoids are two muscle groups used extensively in judo. The forward action of the hands and arms is accomplished by the contraction of these muscles. The pectoralis major contract to move the shoulder girdle forward. The anterior deltoids raise the arm as well as move it forward. Both of these contractions are found in any throwing action to the front side.

Without weights: push-ups, self-resistance, wall push-away
With weights: bench press, incline press

Pulling Action

1: Beginning with the arms against the pad in a full stretch position, this judoka athlete is about to pull forward.

2: His action of driving his arm and shoulder forward is similar to the action found in a tai otoshi or a seoinage.

Multidirectional Pulley Machine

1: Some gyms have a multidirectional pulley machine that can be adjusted to mimic a judo movement.

2: Here, this judoka demonstrates a seoinage- or a tai otoshi-type movement on such a machine.

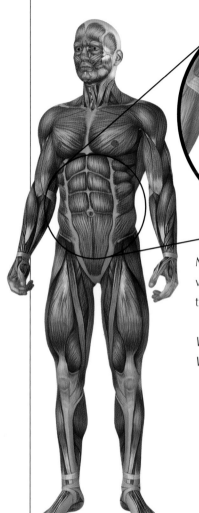

9. *Lower abdomen:*

There are three major sets of stomach muscles that allow us to bend forward or twist at various angles. These muscles include the rectus abdominis, the internal and external obliques, and the transverse abdominis. The oblique muscles wrap around the body and aid in the torque and turn of the torso. (The torque and turn of the oblique muscles has been somewhat addressed in the previous multi-directional machine sequence wherein the pull is joined with turning the body counterclockwise.)

Most judo techniques to various degrees cause the athlete to either contract or pike at the waist to finish a throw off. Also, the stomach is smack dab in the middle of the body and thus influences all other body parts. Therefore, it's sit-up time.

Without weights: sit-ups, crunches, leg raises, buddy-assisted sit-ups, buddy-assisted leg raises
With weights: sit-up machines

Buddy-Assisted Sit-Ups

1: To develop the lower abdomen, have a partner sit on your legs while on the edge of a bench and bend over backward to do your sit-ups.

2: You will find these quite different from doing crunches, which only work the upper abdomen.

Leg Pushdowns

1: Another means of strengthening the abdomen is the plyometric-type leg pushdowns. While lying down, have a partner stand over you with his feet on either side of your head. You hold onto his legs.

2-3: Quickly raise your legs while keeping them straight.

4-5: At the top of your leg raise, have your partner forcefully push them back down.

6: Before your feet hit the floor, raise them and repeat the process. Do these until you have finished your set.

Bench Sit-Ups

Photos by Hayward Nishioka

1: The judoka is on an inclined bench to increase the resistance level.

2-4: If more resistance is needed, he can do sit-ups with a 20-pound weight, do them slower or do more of them. With a little practice, it's possible to do a couple hundred at a time.

10. *Gluteus maximus, minimus, and medius:*

These muscles aid in walking, bending and straightening up, sitting and getting up, and all similar motions found in judo. Of particular interest to the judoka is the ability of this muscle to lift the leg upward to the rear. The techniques of osoto gari and uchimata would greatly benefit from the strengthening of the gluteal muscles.

Without weights: rear leg raises, prone leg raises, buddy-assisted leg raises
With weights: leg-raise machine, rear-leg raise with ankle weights

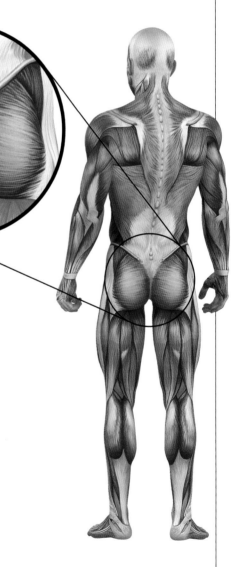

Multi-Hip Machine

Photos by Eric Nishioka

1: The multi-hip machine is well suited for the osoto gari type motion that helps to develop the glutes. With the weights and the position now adjusted, the athlete is ready to kick backwards and upwards.

2-3: The motion should be forcefully executed lifting as high as the machine and your body will allow. Notice that the motion simulates both the osoto gari and the uchimata.

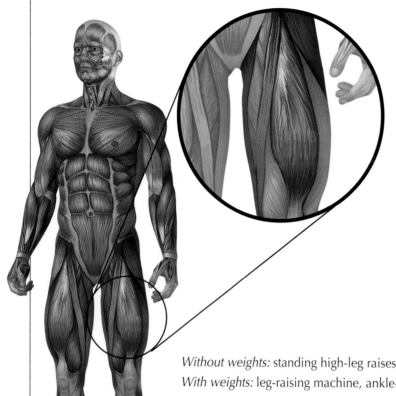

11. *Rectus femoris, sartorius, pectineus, gracilis:*

These are some of the longest muscles in the body and are used to straighten the leg out as well as lift both the upper and lower parts of the leg. Just simple activities like walking, standing, and keeping your balance require the integrated action of all of the leg and hip muscles. For judo, every time you take a step forward or reach out with your leg, you use your leg muscles.

Without weights: standing high-leg raises, self-resistance leg raises, squats, running
With weights: leg-raising machine, ankle-weighted leg raises, leg-extension machine

Leg Raises

1: After adjusting the weights and leg position on the leg-extension machine, the judoka is ready to begin.

2-3: He extends his legs until they are almost fully straight. He then retracts slowly.

Photos by Eric Nishioka

12. *Bicep femoris or hamstring:*

This muscle causes the leg to bend and is helpful in executing the *sankaku jime* leg choke. It is also used by the body for walking, sitting, and standing, and this means that this muscle is vulnerable to cramping and tearing. In the unlikely event of a cramp, merely straighten the leg, grab your toes, and pull them up and back toward your shin while massaging your hamstring.

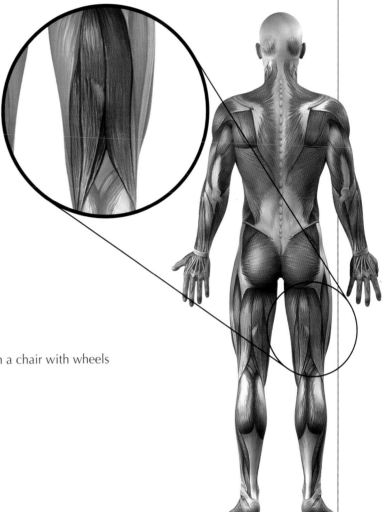

Without weights: move about the room while seated on a chair with wheels
With weights: leg-curl machine

Leg Curls

1: It is best to start out light and build up as you go on this exercise. Here, the judoka practices with light weights and light intensity.

2-3: Once he has warmed up, he proceeds normally.

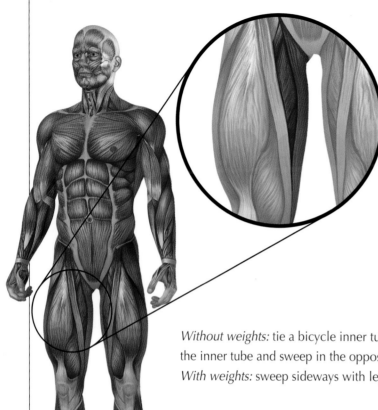

13. *Adductor longus, adductor brevis, gracilis:*

These muscles are found on the inside portion of the leg and help to draw the feet and legs together, which means they are very useful for anyone using an okuri ashi barai.

Without weights: tie a bicycle inner tube to an immovable object, place one foot inside the inner tube and sweep in the opposite direction
With weights: sweep sideways with leg-pulley machine

Multi-Hip Machine

Photos by Eric Nishioka

1: Using the multi-hip machine, the judoka places the inside portion of his leg against the machine and begins to sweep it down and across.

2-3: The sweeping action should go past the supporting foot. As with the foot sweep, extend the foot and hips forward. Note: You may want to alternate using heavy weights, which will give you power, and light weights, which will increase your speed and stamina.

14. *Gastrocnemeous:*

The calf muscles when contracted allow an individual to rise. This is very important for practically every type of throw where the opponent is being loaded—ogoshi, harai goshi, uchimata, seoinage, etc. The muscle is used in the final phase of the throw to get an extra lift off the toes.

Without weights: toe raises, curb-edge toe raises, vertical jumping
With weights: toe-raising machine, squat toe raises, toe presses

Calf-Strengthening Exercise

1: The judoka begins with his toes on the step and his heels down.

2: Next, he flexes and pushes upward against the padded weights. He repeats this action until he is finished with his set.

Chapter Review

1. Discuss how muscles work.
2. List and describe at least five different types of contractions.
3. Explain the difference between circuit training and pyramiding.
4. Discuss the benefits of heavy- and light-weight workouts.
5. Your competitor asks, "Coach, my opponents seem stronger than me. What can I do to not get pushed around so much?" How do you answer?

"Perhaps no one realizes how important a good diet has been for me. I can't describe how important it is. You go along for years weighing too much. Then you change your diet, you start feeling good and you don't even mind looking in the mirror. Gradually, you rise to a different physical and mental level. It reflects on all your life, not just your ability as an athlete.

—Jack Nicklaus, professional golfer, winner of 18 major championships

Nutrition and Weight Management

CHAPTER NINE

Nutrition and Weight Management

"**H**ey coach," Natalie said at practice one day. "Is there anything special I should be taking before competition?" Like many of her fellow judoka, Natalie had heard about all the vitamins, supplements and special energy drinks she could take to maximize her performance.

Across the room, John, the dojo's top competitor, was thinking: I've been cutting weight like crazy and it's taking a toll on me. What should I do?

Queries

1. **What is BMI?**

2. **What is meant by a balanced diet and what's the food pyramid?**

3. **How many calories do I need to consume?**

4. **How about extra vitamins?**

5. **Will ergogenic aids help performance?**

6. **How long before competition should I eat?**

7. **What precautions should I be aware of in cutting weight?**

8. **How fast can I get the weight off without injuring myself?**

9. **What about hydration and rehydration?**

10. **What about heat stroke?**

11. **What about age and gender?**

12. **What about issues of anorexia and bulimia nervosa?**

13. **How much weight can I lose?**

Does any of this sound familiar? If it doesn't, then you need to really start thinking about it. One of the most misunderstood areas of training is that of nutrition and weight management in competition. That's because, though judo coaches and competitors are experts when it comes to techniques and character development, they fall short when it comes to nutritional requirement and competition. This chapter will outline a jumping-off point from which to build a more comprehensive understanding of the subject, as it pertains to judo competition.

What and What Not to Ingest

It is within the nature of athletes to try and maximize their chances of winning. Some athletes intentionally take banned substances in order to optimize their chances of winning. Some athletes unintentionally take banned substances, as suggested by someone like a coach who wants to optimize the athlete's chances of winning. These illicit substances may be drugs, amphetamines, steroids, prescription drugs or even over-the-counter medications that have been banned by the International Olympic Committee. (Yes, there are over-the-counter substances banned by the IOC.) For example, not too many years ago, an athlete ingested a cold medication that he didn't know would show up on his drug test. As a result, he was eliminated from competing in the Olympic Trials.

Rules governing banned substances in organized sports were devised to maintain the high ideals of the Olympics and to create a level playing field on which athletes could complete. It was believed that athletes should compete as a result of their own training and merit rather than have their success depend on some secret elixir.

However, the contemporary win-at-all-costs mentality of sports means that many athletes try to work around the rules, but such an attitude can have detrimental costs. Drugs have long-term side effects. Steroids, protein shakes and even over-the-counter herbal medications are or can be contraindicated. Long-term use of steroids has long been known to cause health problems in athletes who use them for short-term gains. Herbal medications can cause complications when used with prescription drugs or in excessive dosages, all in the name of achieving the best performance.

A well-balanced diet is all that is necessary for any normal person. However, each athlete is slightly different as to his or her physiological needs. Some will consume more than others. Some will take in more carbohydrates, others less fats. Some will not eat any meat, while others can't live without it. Still others will swear by different elixirs, mixtures, multivitamins and minerals that are supposed to enhance performance.

The vitamins and minerals that are necessary for bodily functions can be supplied by a normal intake of fruits and vegetables. Practically all that you eat, be it a hamburger or Cobb salad, is made up of what you need to survive—protein, fats, carbohydrates, vitamins, minerals, water and fiber. All of these nutrients end up as chime in the stomach, then travel through the small intestine, where fingerlike projections lining the intestine draw up the nutrients into the blood vessels. The nutrients are transported through the liver where they are further broken down and filtered before being distributed throughout the body.

As was mentioned, a balanced diet differs from athlete to athlete and athletic event to athletic event as to amount and type of food. Nonetheless, the source from which the nutrients are derived is the same, which is what you eat. In all, athletes may consume between 2,000 and 3,500 calories a day depending on bodily needs. The larger, more active athletes will usually consume more calories than smaller less active ones. (Calories are the units of energy found in the foods that we eat. In Europe, and even in the United States, they are measured in "grams.")

The only nutrients that truly act as fuel for the body are the macronutrients—like protein, carbohydrates and fats. Micronutrients like vitamins and minerals help to rebuild and regulate bodily functions. Water and fiber aid in the promotion of bodily functions as well.

Macronutrients

Macronutrients are sometimes referred to as fuelers because they are nutrients that provide the body with energy. The first macronutrient we'll look at is the protein, followed by the carbohydrate and fat.

Protein means "of first importance." Proteins are made up of about 20 amino acids, 11 of which can be produced by humans. This means that you can't make nine of these amino acids, which is why you must ingest them from outside sources. These nine amino acids are termed as essential amino acids. Together with the other 11, the 20 amino acids make up a complete protein.

The nine amino acids that you need to ingest are usually found in various types of animal products, like meat, fish, eggs, cheese, etc. They may also be found in plant-based foods, but specific plants usually do not form a complete protein the way humans do. Plants also need to use outside sources to collect the necessary amino acids for proper growth and development to occur. There are ways to combine two or more plants in order to produce a complete protein, e.g., rice and beans, but nutritionists generally agree that the quality and quantity of plant protein is not sufficient or equal to that of animal products. They also suggest that approximately 10 percent of your diet should consist of proteins.

Why? Well, proteins are important in that they make up your muscle tissue. They also, to a degree, restore and maintain growth of healthy tissue. Some studies have been conducted indicating that protein is necessary for optimal performance and can delay the onset of fatigue during extended bouts of exercise. Protein deficiency is something athletes who are vegetarians might have to watch out for because of the nature of their diets.

If protein does all that, what do carbohydrates do? Carbohydrates are the best source of energy for athletes and should make up 60 percent of the athlete's diet. Years ago, it was believed by a number of nutritionists that in order to lose weight and be healthy, you should cut back on carbohydrates. In the 2000s, this idea has been reversed. Now, athletes in strenuous activities carbo-load around the day before the event. Of course for judo, there is the issue of trying to make weight. You may want to hold off on the carbo-loading unless you're a heavyweight.

There are three types of carbohydrates: monosaccharides, disaccharides and polysaccharides. A monosaccharide is a simple sugar, like glucose, fructose, or galactose. Think of monosaccharides as grapes or fruit juice; they are simple because they contain refined sugar and few essential vitamins, which means they are easier to digest. A disaccharide, at its simplest, is technically just two monosaccharides put together. It includes brown sugar, maple syrup, honey and high-fructose corn syrup. A polysaccharide is a complex carbohydrate that includes grains and staples such as wheat, beans, soybeans, potatoes, rice, corn and sorghum. Polysaccharides are complex because they are rich with essential vitamins and minerals and take longer to digest. The polysaccharide sector also includes vegetables such as lettuce, cabbage, tomatoes, celery, onions and broccoli. Because these polysaccharides tend to have insoluble fibers, they are sometimes classified as fibers. These are all natural products that judoka should be ingesting on a regular basis.

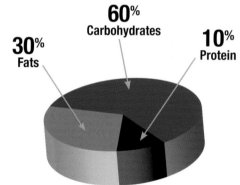

If proteins make up 10 percent of your diet and carbohydrates 60 percent, then fats should make up the difference and account for approximately 30 percent of your intake.

There are two important reasons why fat intake is important. The first reason is that fats are necessary to absorb fat-soluble vitamins like A, D, E and K. The second reason is that fats are a high-density energy source that contains nine calories per gram rather than the four calories per gram in proteins and carbohydrates. This means that fats take longer to kick in and burn as an energy source, which is vital in extended energy-consumption events like long randori sessions or all-day tournaments where there is little time to eat or properly digest a full meal.

In light of the fact that eating fatty food is usually considered bad, 30 percent may seem high, but this all depends on the types of fats you consume. There are three types of fats: saturated, unsaturated and polyunsaturated. Saturated fats are animal fats and will solidify at room temperature. They consist of items like butter and lard. Unsaturated fats are made up of vegetable oils like corn, sunflower, safflower, canola, soy, nut and olive oil. Polyunsaturated fats may be found in fish oils and specially manufactured products termed trans-fats. These are usually vegetable oils that have been hydrogenated. Hydrogenation is a process by which hydrogen is processed into normally liquid vegetable oils, thus making them into a solid for commercial advantage. Studies indicate that overconsumption of trans-fats has a detrimental effect on the cardiovascular system and health. However, underutilization of fats can cause vitamin deficiencies, which will affect your judo performance. So what do you do?

Try to avoid trans-fats. Try to avoid overingestion of saturated fats. Be aware of hidden fats such as coconut oils, palm oils, hydrogenated oils, and other synthesized fats like olestra and margarine in fast foods. Do not try to completely eliminate fats from your diet, which can be especially detrimental for active women athletes and for children during their developmental years.

Micronutrients

Vitamins are important to almost every bodily function but are only needed in very small quantities. As a general rule, if you are eating a balanced diet, you are probably ingesting the "RDA" of vitamins necessary to maintain a healthy body. RDA stands for Recommended Dietary Allowances, the amount an individual should be consuming daily as established by the Food and Nutrition Board of the U.S. National Academy of Sciences. Another general rule: Unless there is an obvious deficiency, you do not need to take megadoses of vitamin supplements. In many instances, extra vitamins can cause health problems such as hypervitaminosis and other chemical imbalances in the body, especially common with fat-soluble vitamins. Nutritionists suggest that diets rich in fruits and vegetables are the ticket to antioxidants that fight heart problems and cancer—good information to have, as such health issues complicate the judo lifestyle.

Minerals are important in building tissue like muscles and bones, but also in maintaining important bodily functions like the regulation of metabolic processes—i.e., digestion. As you learned in the macronutrient section, you take in minerals through outside plant or animal sources. When consumed, these outside sources are turned into metalloenzymes, ions, and electrolytes that carry an electrical charge. These regulate things like muscle contractions, nerve impulses, acid/base balance, water in our system, and the heartbeat.

Minerals are just like those found on a periodic table. You consume certain elements found on the periodic table. Of the minerals people ingest, there are two basic categories: major and trace. Major minerals are those like sodium, chloride, potassium and sulfate. The major mineral phosphorous is the second most abundant mineral in the human body while magnesium, which is mostly found in bone, barely qualifies as a major mineral. The most well-known major mineral is calcium, which is essential to a number of biological systems—skeletal, muscular, digestive, cardiovascular—and supports the function and synthesis of red blood cells. Trace minerals are called "trace" because the body only needs a very small amount. Generally, a normal diet supplies enough to maintain health, but if you're missing one of them, your body will know it. Trace minerals include iron, zinc, iodine, selenium, copper, manganese, fluoride, chromium and molybedenum. The minerals you need, both major and trace, are found in numerous foods like bananas, potatoes, oranges, broccoli, tomatoes, onions, meats, and eggs.

For judo specifically, proper vitamin and mineral intake helps with neural—neuron to neuron—transmissions. Neurons travel from head to toe in order to tell the body what to do—when to attack with an ouchi gari or defend by bending the knees. All this happens in a blink of an eye because of transmitter chemicals like acetylcholine, acetylcholinesterase, epinephrine, serotonin and dopamine, all of which are products of vitamins and minerals.

Water and Fiber

While water doesn't supply caloric content, it is absolutely necessary as a medium by which digestion and life can be sustained. The body is 60 percent water, after all! Under ideal conditions, a

True/False

human can probably last a week or so with little water in his or her system. Under adverse conditions, a human will last little more than a day.

You are constantly losing water through evaporation, respiration and excretion and must replenish your body's supply for it to properly function. (You've probably heard that it's a good idea to drink eight glasses of water a day.) If you have ingested enough water, then your pH (acid/base) is in balance and digestion and elimination of wastes run smoothly. A simple test to see if you're drinking enough water is to check the color of your urine. If it is yellow to dark yellow, you need to ingest more water. You want your urine to be clear or nearly so because it will ensure sodium and electrolytes are balanced and, for athletes, that there is an adequate supply of energy to combat fatigue. Water also regulates our senses and our body temperature.

Non-nutritive fiber generally comes from indigestible carbohydrates found in leafy vegetables, plants, fruit skins, pulp, and some manufactured grains and cereals such as bran. Corn is a good example of a non-nutritive fiber that we can readily see in our waste materials. These foodstuffs help to give body and form to an otherwise aqueous substance that would flow too quickly through our digestive tract and not allow proper absorption and digestion, especially of fats and good cholesterol. Furthermore, fiber aids in the prevention of constipation, diabetes, and diverticulosis, which any judoka wants to avoid.

Weight-Management Problems and Competition

With all the information science has revealed about diet and nutrition, statistics show that modern society is moving toward a trend of having larger bodies at an earlier age. The most touted culprit is the prevalence of high-fat and high-salt foods as well as overconsumption of these foods. Food additives, like high-fructose corn syrup, are used in many food products as a sweetener and preservative. However, because the body does not digest all of the additives' molecules, the excess is stored in body fat.

The National Institutes of Health advises Americans to monitor their BMI or Body Mass Index. BMI is based on age and height and allows a person to determine body-fat level as compared to what is the generally accepted leve for his or her age and height group. People with higher levels are probably at greater risk of heart problems, cancer and diabetes. As an active competitor, you might find that the chart is a little off because your muscle mass will make you heavier. (The first BMI charts were standardized by the Metropolitan Life Insurance Company and did not take athletic builds into consideration; rather they based their data on the average person.)

Weight management is still an issue for the judoka because of weight categories for competition. The coach and competitor need to learn how to navigate through this portal safely.

There are a number of reasons that judoka pay attention to weight categories and try to cut weight:

1. The competition seems easier in the next division down.

2. There are not as many competitors in the next division down.

3. The spot at your current weight is already filled by your teammate and the coach wants you to fill in at the lower weight. Besides, you only have a few pounds to lose to make weight.

These reasons seem all well and good, but what do you do if you have a lot of weight to lose in a short amount of time?

Many nutritionists and health professionals suggest that safe weight reduction is no more than two pounds per week, but even this number is dependent on a competitor's age, height and weight. The age factor is usually not figured in on the BMI chart that formulates a height-to-weight ratio showing a mathematical correlation to how much fat a person has. The BMI chart, in addition to only catering to the average adult and no children, does not take into consideration heavily muscled athletes. Coaches and competitors instead should just use it to think: "Ah ha! This is my starting point for what's considered 'normal.'"

Using the BMI chart as a guideline, we can see that taller and heavier individuals can lose more weight without dire consequences. Generally, the shorter and lighter the individual, the less margin of safety he has as he loses pounds. Thus a 225-pound judoka wishing to get down to the next lower weight class would have to lose five pounds. Using the safe model of losing two pounds per week, five pounds should take about two-and-a-half weeks. Now let's look at someone wanting to go from 137 pounds to 132 pounds. He would have to lose a greater percentage of his body weight than

In team and "winner stay up" tournaments, the old idea of the smaller man beating the larger is still a reality. However, because of modern weight divisions, there are now health considerations. In this team match, the smaller judoka played the edge and executed an unexpected left-sided throw, thus beating his larger opponent.

the 225-pound judoka. Lighter individuals usually have less fat to burn off than heavier athletes; consequently they tend to burn more carbohydrates and proteins. The heavier and taller person will generally have more weight to "play with" than the smaller individual.

Athletes and Nutritional Issues

While cutting weight is beneficial in an athletic sense, it is detrimental in the long run. Of course, this book is meant to help you maximize your performance, but both competitor and coach need to give some thought to the long-term effects of training for competition.

Some of those issues are:

1. ***Children and weight control:*** When children are told to cut weight in order to enter a lower weight division, coaches and parents need to remember several things. First of all, if a child is young and light in weight already, he or she will give up a greater percentage of body fat. Thus, a 10-year-old heavyweight, weighing in at 100 pounds, is recommended to drop two pounds to fight in a lower-weight division. Two pounds only make up two percent of the athlete's body weight, which is not a lot at all. In contrast, it is not advisable for a coach to tell a 78-pound eight-year-old heavyweight to lose the same amount because the competitor is younger, lighter and in his growth phase. The first two decades of life are major development years for humans. Long-term deprivation of much-needed nutrients during these years may result in physical and psychological damage to young people. Director of the Metabolic and Body Composition Laboratory in Oklahoma, Jeffrey Stout, Ph.D, warns that children require 20 to 30 percent more energy than adults and more protein consumption. The French judo model is to encourage body movements until the age of 13 in various modalities; the honing of techniques of various types both left and right, standing and on the ground; sportsmanship; gamesmanship; and enjoyment of our challenging sport of judo. There is very little if any national effort to develop or discover a "tiny tot" champion. Things begin to change after the age of 13 but only for selected individuals under tight supervision.

Vegan/Vegetarian Athletes

Some competitors restrict themselves to a nonmeat-based diet or one that does not allow the intake of any animal products or byproducts. Their nutrition instead comes mainly from plant-based sources. These athletes have to be extra vigilant about consuming enough protein because vegetarian diets do not provide as much protein as those that include meat products. Meat is a more densely packed protein source. Thus, vegetarian athletes may find they have to supplement their diets with vitamins E6 and B12, calcium, iron and others. Seek the advice of a professional to find out what you may need. Complementary proteins are another means of making a complete protein. This is done by consuming certain carbohydrates which, when added together, supply the necessary amino acids to make a protein like the previously mentioned rice and beans.

2. *Female athlete triad:* Because coaches and competitors focus so intently on training effectively for competition, they don't always think about how a simple suggestion to "lose a few pounds" can bring about detrimental effects such as "female athlete triad." Female athlete triad is characterized by disordered eating, amenorrhea and osteoporosis. The syndrome affects competitors who are counting calories and drastically reducing their nutrients to cut weight. The interesting thing is they are not cutting weight for appearance but to improve athletic performance. In the process, they develop such low fat content, they are unable to produce estrogen, which leads to amenorrhea or irregular menstruation. Low intake of trace minerals like iron leads to osteoporosis, even in female competitors of a young age. Nutritionists will often suggest the taking of extra calcium and iron supplements, especially for adolescents and young adults in serious training.

3. *Anorexia nervosa/bulimia nervosa:* These well-known eating disorders are related to female athlete triad, but their motivations are very different. In anorexia nervosa, the individual is intensely afraid of gaining weight because of a distorted self-image. This misperception causes people to deprive their bodies of food, even if they are 85 percent below the healthy body weight for their age and height. (Female sufferers of anorexia can also experience amenorrhea because they are lacking certain nutrients.) Bulimia nervosa is a condition in which the individual will try to keep his or her weight down while still enjoying food. There are different types of bulimia, but basically, the individual will consume usually large amounts of food, then regurgitate or use laxatives to rid themselves of the ingested foodstuffs. Sometimes referred to

as "binging and purging," this practice can have dire consequences on the teeth, throat and breath because the acid used in the stomach to digest food can erode the teeth and body tissue after vomiting. A practice similar to binging and purging but not as harmful is that of chewing one's food but swallowing only the juices and spitting out the remains.

4. *Cutting water weight:* Because the body is made up of so much water, many competitors will try to cut their water weight. Water weighs 62.4 pounds per square foot. The well-known practice of consuming eight glasses of water a day shows how much water the human body needs to function properly. To cut weight, competitors will forgo any water for a day or so, generally right before competition, so when they weigh in, their weight is drastically lower. During hot summer days, time should be allotted for intermittent hydration periods, and athletes should be encouraged to hydrate often. During extra hot days, practices may even be canceled. Coaches should be mindful of those cutting weight, in poor physical condition, or having any health issues. Confusion, vertigo, or loss of energy can be indications of more serious problems to come.

5. *Overhydrating/overeating:* Another issue that goes hand-in-hand with cutting water weight is overhydrating and overeating. After having made weight, the competitor will overcompensate for his starvation diet and drink or eat too much, with just minutes to go before the start of a match. Instead, encourage eating and drinking in moderation to prevent a bloated feeling before going into a match. Allow a couple hours for food to digest so the body doesn't have to work so hard on the process of digestion. Instead, it can devote its time to the muscle tissues. Ideally, though, a competitor and coach should strive not to find themselves in this situation. When helping their competitors lose weight, coaches should be aware of whether the individual judoka has a precondition, limitations, history of eating disorders, etc.

Input and Output

So, how do competitors lose weight in a healthy way? First, start early and give yourself plenty of time to cut weight. The more you want to cut, the longer you should allow for losing the weight.

Your weight is controlled by two factors: your input, or how much food you put into your system, and your output, or how much energy you expend. To measure your input vs. output, log all the calories predicted in your food sources to see how many calories are needed to finish your day, feel reasonably healthy and maintain the same weight. (The average adult male will consume around 2,000 calories a day.) Considering that a good-size American hamburger contains about 500 calories, you theoretically could use up your daily allotment fairly quickly. (Don't forget to add in the fries and soft drink laden with high-fructose corn syrup. Add in a dessert, and you're over the 1,000-calorie mark!) How do we use up these calories?

Fortunately, judoka expend a lot of calories and energy so

True/False

1. **Losing weight is often motivated by easier competition in a lower weight division.**

2. **Nutritionists have no suggestions as to how much weight can be taken off.**

3. **The BMI is the best indicator of what weight division a judoka should be in.**

4. **Basically, your weight is determined by what and how much you eat.**

5. **When cutting weight, plans should be made months ahead of a competition.**

Answers: 1.T, 2.F, 3.F, 4.T, 5.T

a judoka's metabolism rate is a lot faster than the ordinary person's. According to James Michener's book, *Sports in America*, judo is listed as number eight on a scale of one to 10 of the toughest sports in the world. The Tour de France is listed at 10. Brian Sharkey, the author of *Physiology of Fitness*, listed judo as expending 13 calories per minute and soccer at nine cal/min. Therefore, 45 minutes of randori practice could yield a 585-calorie expenditure. This amount added to the various activities you engage in during the day, such as work, chores and even eating, digesting, and sleeping, can theoretically use up the 2,000 calories you ingest daily. It is when the amount of calories expended exceeds the number ingested that the body begins to go into its reserves; the liver will begin converting its stores of fats, carbohydrates and proteins into glucose or blood sugar. The fewer calories left at the end of the day, the less weight you gain. A deficit of a thousand calories a day can yield a two-pound reduction in weight. The problem with this formula is that most people try to cut the deficit by cutting the intake side rather than increasing the output side of the equation. It would be foolish to fall below 1,000 calories a day for an athlete in a highly competitive sport like judo, for which an element of strength has to be maintained, not to mention the health hazards that can come from reducing nutrients your body needs.

At this point it should be mentioned that there are many in the reading audience who have witnessed athletes in extreme weight-loss situations This author once coached an athlete who was 11 pounds overweight when arriving at the tournament site. The weigh-ins were beginning in five

Dietary Suggestions

1. **Increase consumption of fruits and vegetables.**

2. **Eat in moderation and avoid late-night meals.**

3. **Eat more meals but in less volume.**

4. **Avoid fried and saturated fatty foods.**

5. **Read food labels and avoid high-fructose corn syrup.**

6. **Don't overcook your vegetables.**

7. **Use the food pyramid as a guide to healthy eating.**

8. **Eat more colorful home-cooked meals.**

9. **Keep a diary of what your caloric intake is from carbohydrates, fats and proteins. Remember 60, 30 and 10 percents respectively.**

10. **Include in your diary the amount of exercise and approximate calories burned.**

11. **Keep hydrated, especially during hot summer days.**

12. **Avoid banned substances and steroids.**

hours. The player said, "Don't worry coach, I'll make weight." With plastic sweats, a towel, a jump rope and a credit card, he went into a sauna, skipped rope, periodically stepped out of the sauna, dried off his suit with the towel and stroked off all the sweat with a credit card. Then he jumped back in to repeat the process over and over till he had lost the requisite weight. Yes, the athlete lost 11 pounds in less than five hours. What was even more amazing was that he went on the next day to become the lightest man ever to win the U.S. Grand Championships, and his name is Pat Burris.

Most of his ability to lose weight came from his background in wrestling, in which wrestlers are constantly cutting extreme amounts of weight on a regular basis and building a tolerance for such practices. Also, this is water weight and it is not uncommon for judoka to lose four to six pounds of water weight during practice. But, unlike at a weigh-in, at practice you have time to rehydrate.

Extreme water loss for normal people can cause nausea, weakness, stress, and dizziness due to the lack of electrolytes. This is in no way an endorsement of this type of practice; it is merely stating what seems to be common in competitive sports. A practice with some forethought and planning can be changed to a more reasonable model of weight reduction without the risk of losing strength and stamina at competition time.

Chapter Review

1. Discuss some of the banned-substance issues listed earlier.
2. List the six nutrients.
3. Discuss why fats are a necessary part of our diet.
4. Discuss the possible problems associated with weight loss in children and women.
5. Discuss what must be done to safely lose weight.

"What you don't want are serious injuries. When you're injured, you can't practice, and when you can't practice, you can't get better."

—Gene LeBell, national judo champion, coach, actor, author

Dealing With Injury

CHAPTER 10

Dealing With Injury

During randori, Dennis is frustrated by the two previous attacks his opponent Mario successfully executed on him. He musters up all his pent-up anger and unleashes a fast left tai otoshi against his larger opponent. Mario's defenses are usually pretty good, but he's caught off guard by Dennis's sudden tai otoshi. Besides, he's never even seen Dennis do a tai otoshi. In an attempt to avoid the throw, Dennis tries to post out his left arm. As his outstretched hand tries to brace his falling body, Mario hears a snap! Everyone in the dojo stops their practice and looks to the sound of the awkward fall. They are quiet. Mario looks in disbelief at his hand. There is no pain, at least not yet, but the sight makes him feel nauseated. As if in a bad dream, he sees that all his fingers are correctly extended except for one—his middle finger is helplessly out of place at a 90-degree angle. The dojo is quiet. No one seems to know what to do. What would you do?

Injuries occur when parts of the body are stressed beyond their ability to maintain integrity. This loss of integrity may manifest itself in the form of pain or various degrees of loss of function. The excessive stresses may be felt internally or externally. External injuries may be caused by coming in contact with another body or object at high speed. The point of impact may be against an area that is anatomically weak, e.g., a blunt-object strike to the eye, a body hitting the knee at the wrong angle or the body landing on a hard object. Internal damage may include muscle tears; hernia; ligament, meniscus and tendon problems; stress fractures; genetic weakness of an internal organ; temperature problems aggravated by dehydration; or even contracting of a pathogen.

Queries

1. **Are you ready in case of an emergency?**

2. **What are some things you can do to have a safer judo environment?**

3. **How can coaches best prepare athletes for safer judo practice?**

4. **What should you do in the event of an injury?**

5. **What is taping and strapping?**

It's common knowledge that injuries do occur in athletic endeavors. It is also a fact that a physician is not always present at all athletic events and practice sessions to diagnose and treat an injury. Fortunately, there are several things that competitors can do to avoid injuries and that coaches can make sure their athletes do to prevent injuries. There are also steps that competitors and coaches can take to alleviate the pain of an injury with a little training in first aid.

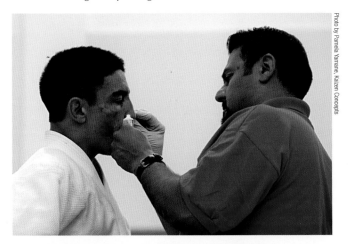

Photo by Pamela Yamane, Kaizen Concepts

Sanctioned tournaments are required to have professionals to assist if minor athletic injuries arise. Nose bleeds must be attended to immediately.

Warm-Up and Stretching Exercises

In addition to maintaining a safe and clean environment to work out in, properly preparing the body for a workout session is key. It is best to prepare by lightly stressing those body parts that will be most used during your training session with warm-up exercises. Generally, begin with easier types of exercises and end with harder types of exercises. For example, begin with push-ups, light jogging, etc., to warm up your core temperature instead of doing 100 crunches right off the bat. During hot summer months, however, be mindful of heat exhaustion or worse, like heat stroke, because the body will heat up faster, especially during exhaustive workouts. If you feel or look disoriented, excessively weak, dizzy or nauseated during practice, rest on the side in a cool location. Hydrating with water before, during and after training is also a good practice and helps in avoiding overheating problems.

Stretching before and after working out is of particular importance. A limber person has a wider range of motion, which gives that competitor advantages over one who is not. For example, a competitor needs to lift his legs into the air for an uchimata in order to throw the opponent. The more the competitor can stretch his leg up, the more extra lift he'll get to throw the opponent.

There are two major ways to stretch: static and ballistic. Static stretching is when you stretch the muscle slowly until you feel it stretch to its maximum point. When you reach that point, hold the position for five to 25 seconds; repeat the motion three to five times. You

For coaches, there are several things you may do to prevent injuries from happening. First, stress the importance of safety in the dojo to your students. Although a student should know what is acceptable and what is not acceptable behavior in the _dojo_, you should remind the athletes of safe and unsafe practices from time to time. Usually, the best time is before or after practice.

should see an increase in range of motion. Ballistic stretching employs a bouncing rhythmic action to which you alternate stretching with relaxing. Static stretching allows muscle fibers to relax and elongate more effectively than ballistic stretching that, when used to achieve the same results, can cause muscle-fiber tears.

Judo inherently employs ballistic movements, and the partial intent of calisthenics is to ready the competitor's body for the rigors of practice. Thus, ballistic stretching should definitely be part of your routine. However, it would probably be wiser to begin with a set or two of static stretches before "going ballistic."

PNF, which stands for proprioceptive neuromuscular facilitation, stretching is also a nice alternative to static stretching, but you need to have a good partner. In PNF exercises, one partner stretches while the other facilitates that person's stretching. For example, an athlete is seated on the floor with his legs apart and stretched in front of him. He reaches his arms and back forward as far as he can go, then his partner pushes from behind until the athlete says stop. The athlete holds the position for five to 10 seconds before he relaxes. There are many other PNF-type stretching exercises, but remember that they should not be done without a good partner who has had some training in this type of stretching.

Once you have raised your core temperature, start with warm-up requiring muscle contractions like sit-ups and push-ups, etc. Now you are ready for those types of warm-ups that require odd positions, and intensity level changes, plyometrics, and judo-specific exercises. (In some dojo, stretching is part of the warm-up exercises.) A note of caution for the older competitor: Give more attention and time to warming up. This will aid in preventing injuries, which means more time for quality, injury-free practice sessions to improve your skills.

Proper Form

Another important way to prevent injuries is to pay close attention to the selection and proper execution of techniques. The competitor's physical makeup should be a consideration. Fit the techniques to the athlete's body type. For example, taller competitors have a more difficult time in executing a morote seoinage or a sode tsurikomi goshi because they are techniques that require getting under the opponent. It would be more prudent to have the taller athlete add an osoto gari or a harai goshi to his family of techniques, to take advantage of his longer reach.

When techniques are practiced and entered into correctly, the chances of an injury happening to the uke or tori are not as great.

When training for a technique, it is more important to have correct form than to execute a technique speedily. For example, when a technique is executed correctly, it seems effortless. That's because foot positioning is correctly done. As your feet are getting into position, your hands are pulling the opponent off-balance. Your center of gravity is placed under his because your knees are bent. Your body is turning in to the opponent, and the torque from your spinning body has popped him into the air. As the opponent is lifted by the extension of your knees, you continue to turn, then finish a well-executed throw. If any of these elements are missing even to a small degree, you will be out of alignment when you execute the throw, making it difficult to finish. In some cases, your incorrect position may even help the opponent counter your action or, worse yet, cause you to strain a body part in your attempt.

Before Competition

Give-and-take cooperative throwing drills, entry drills, mental practice or watching and studying judo videos are methods of practicing judo skills that also cut down on injuries. As a coach, you may want to use these types of practices before a major event, when injuries inconveniently seem to occur because a competitor is overeager to make whatever improvements are possible before the big event. As discussed in Chapter 2, it is usually best to start cutting down on the intense randori sessions the closer your competitor gets to tournament time. In fact, you may cut back as early as a week before so that the competitor is not even working out except for uchikomi and nagekomi practice. This practice of cutting back on heavy workouts is known as "tapering down," or just "tapering." This also helps the competitor rebuild energy stores, as discussed in Chapter 9.

In some cases, if your athlete has a history of injuries before tournaments, exclude working out at least two days prior to the event.

Strength Building

Strengthening body parts prior to the practicing of certain techniques is another way to avoid injuries. In particular, wrists, ankles, shoulders, elbows, knees and neck are areas that bend, twist and rotate. They are often vital to the execution of many judo techniques. Enlarging and increasing the musculature and strength in these areas gives added support to the joints, and helps reduce the possibility of injuries. For added information, study Chapter 8 on weight-lifting and resistance training.

Sparring

Of course, the ultimate way to prevent serious injuries is to not engage in hard practice sessions or tournament play. Sometimes this is the best option, especially if the competitor has a new or serious recurring injury. Another less drastic alternative to stopping all judo practices is to engage in half randori. In half randori, the training partners attack and resist but with a slight twist: There is entry into a technique but no throwing of the opponent. Thus, you have

True/False

1. Injuries can occur as a result of faulty selection and execution of techniques.

2. In judo, speed is the most important attribute of a technique.

3. Injury prevention can be enhanced by strengthening the body.

4. Selection of different modes of practice can lower injury rates.

5. Tapering increases the possibility of injury while decreasing skill level.

Answers: 1.T, 2.F, 3.T, 4.T, 5.F

—— Injury-Prevention Preparation for Coaches ——

As a coach, you will confront questions like: I feel faint, should I continue working out? Or, I only have a minute left and I'm ahead, but my shoulder is killing me. What should I do? Or, my elbow is recovering from a hyperextension; can you wrap it for me because my match is next?

How will you respond? If there is no one else around, you need to have the answers. That's why there are a few things that should always be on the stellar coach's checklist:

1. Have a check-off list of possible pre-existing health conditions that you should be aware of as a coach. A personal history questionnaire of the competitor is a good place to start.

2. If your competitor hasn't engaged in any physical activity for some time and/or is an older athlete, have him get a physician's OK and keep it on file. Update it periodically.

3. If you haven't done so already, take a class in first aid/CPR.

4. Take a taping-and-strapping class.

5. Have a first-aid kit available and keep it up to date. Also keep your knowledge of all its contents fresh in your mind.

6. Have a "what if" list. Go over it with your students. It should include things to do in case of an emergency: contact persons, local hospitals, police, 911, etc., during training hours or for a competition.

7. Have competitors, or the competitor's guardian, sign a waiver that shows they recognize the possible dangers of judo competition. Make sure you also sit down and talk with them—competitors, parents, minors, etc.—so they understand what they are signing.

8. Of course, know your athlete, his or her likes, dislikes and condition.

"half" randori. In doing half randori, the competitors work on improving their timing when entering a technique. Without the throws, the danger of injury or re-injury is dramatically lessened.

When practiced by beginners, randori can turn into an escalation of effort that employs all-out throws. For example, a beginner throws his fellow judoka in randori. That thrown judoka thinks the following: OK, I'll get you back. So he tries even harder to throw the original beginner. Now that beginner starts to think: Throw me, will you! Take that! The beginner dumps his fellow judoka even harder. In this type of escalation, there is a greater likelihood of injury. In contrast, advanced players usually "get it;" there is no ego for them during randori. They learn to balance that subtle line between grace and aggression. Thus, they get to enjoy the feel of a well-executed throw, avoid unnecessary injuries, and improve their performance.

When Injury Strikes

Injuries can be internally or externally initiated. Internal injuries can result due to a genetic weakness, wear and tear of a limb or ligament, or as a result of the aging process. Coming into contact with objects can cause external injuries like abrasions, cuts, punctures, blunt-force traumas, sprains, strains, broken bones and internal-organ damage. At sanctioned tournaments, there is usually a staff of medical help with training beyond basic first aid. However, most injuries at the dojo level are dealt with by concerned nonprofessionals. It is these injuries, if not treated properly, that can become a concern when preparing for or participating in a competition.

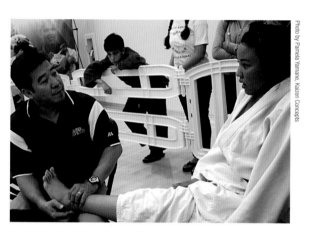

Professionals at tournaments take the guesswork out of injuries. They are trained to diagnose and give you advice. Dojo settings don't always have the luxury of a professional on site. Generally, they rely on the first provider.

If he is fortunate, the competitor injured at a dojo will be attended by a person trained in basic first aid. (Currently, it is strongly recommended for liability reasons that coaches be certified in CPR and first aid, however it is not mandatory.) In any event, a first provider of aid will follow some basic rules, which may include RICE.

RICE is a mnemonic or memory device to remember methods of dealing with injuries. "R" is for rest, "I" for ice, "C" for compression and "E" for elevation, thus RICE.

1. ***Rest:*** Every competitor has a different tolerance level for pain and hard work. Some coaches tell their athletes to work through an injury while others do not allow their athletes on the mat unless they are 100-percent recovered. Competitors often hear coaches say, "Come on, tough it out!" Other coaches feel that certain injuries are an indication that the athlete is subconsciously at or near his tolerance level and that his body may need a rest for even minor injuries. For some athletes, injuries are a hedge against losing. "Coach, I lost because of my injury." Or should he happen to win, "Coach, I won in spite of my injury." Only the player knows how he really feels. The athlete should know if he is really hurt, and if he is, he should be dissuaded from practicing or competing. Much is dependent on the injury and weighing it against the importance of the event. Confronted with a choice between resting a sprained ankle and fighting a final match at the Olympics Games? The match seems a more likely choice, of course. Resting a sprained ankle or going to practice prior to a tournament? Maybe a rest is in order. For young children there is always time, and their health should be primary in the coach's mind.

2. ***Ice:*** Ice is the next thing to consider for an inflammatory injury, be it temporary or chronic. Ice is a vasoconstrictor that impedes the flow of blood pooling to an impacted area. Too much blood

to an area is not only uncomfortable but restricts movement, especially around joints that swell. In the event of an injury like a sprain or even a blunt trauma, it may be advisable to pack the area with a cold pack or a compress of crushed ice wrapped in a piece of cloth or towel. Usually ice should be applied about 20 minutes on and 20 minutes off. Repeating the process three or four times might be needed. Some professional athletes will even ice affected areas prior to a practice or a meet. Motrin, Advil, and other anti-inflammatory medications may also be used in conjunction with ice. However, for prolonged use of even over-the-counter medications, one should consult with a professional about possible unwanted side effects. You may also want to check the competition rules for banned substances to see if the drug is allowable.

3. *Compression:* "C" stands for compression. While this is generally applied to cuts, puncture wounds, a tear in the skin or an abrasion, it may also be used to stop some nose bleeds by pinching the nose and tilting the head back for a few minutes. Because of the possibility of bloodborne infections, protective rubber or latex gloves should be worn. All blood-contacted items should be properly disposed of as well. It may also be a good idea to have handy a 10- to 15-percent bleach solution to spray on all affected areas.

4. *Elevation:* The last letter, "E," is for elevation. Any affected area below the heart is subject to blood pooling. This is usually the case with the knees, ankles, and toes but can also apply to elbows, wrists and fingers. For relief, you need only sit or lay down and raise the affected area higher than the heart.

Wrapping, Strapping and Taping

In the event of a possible sprain or strain, it is always best to determine the extent of the injury before continuing a practice or a match. If the athlete feels excessive pain or an inability to move a particular bone or joint, he should be referred to a professional for further examination and care. While a compound fracture is highly unlikely, it would be best to call 911 for help, but if immediate attention is dependent on you, splint the area before transporting the individual to a medical facility. For dislocations, reduce the injury by packing it in ice, properly wrapping the area and taking the athlete to a medical facility.

To tape and strap the individual, you will need one-and-a-half-inch athletic tape and pre-wrap.

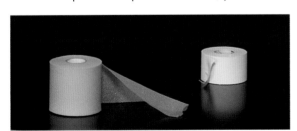

Pre-wrap (left) is thinner than nylon film. It is used before taping to prevent chafing, which occurs if athletic tape is placed directly on the skin's surface.

These can be purchased at most sporting goods stores or online. Cramer, Johnson & Johnson, and Mueller are some of the larger suppliers to choose from for bulk purchasing. While the tape does the trick in regards to supporting an injured limb, pre-wrap prevents direct contact of the tape to the skin, which can otherwise cause irritation and blistering. It is a thin film placed over the area before you apply the tape to the injury.

When dealing with athletic tape, you will need to know how to cut the tape into usable strips. While you can always use scissors, it's easier to just tear the tape. Hold the tape at the edge tightly between the fingers and thumb. To tear the tape, quickly push down with one hand while pulling up with the other. If you are not successful at tearing the tape, you may have to relocate your fingers to a different spot and try again.

The following examples of wrapping and strapping are used for recovering injuries and/or areas that need support in order to prevent further injury. This section covers the areas that are most commonly injured in judo, such as:

1. **Fingers:** Sprained fingers can be caused by a jamming or twisting action to one or more of the hand digits. Splinting a finger with a hard wood or metal object may prevent you from getting a proper grip. The splint could also cause injury to your opponent, whether in training or competition. That's why wrapping and strapping is the better way to go. You'll support the hurt finger by taping it to an adjacent and unhurt digit. Note: Generally, there's no need to use pre-wrap for digits, but it can be applied to hairier limbs, like the hands and arms.

2. **Thumbs:** Jammed thumbs are another type of injury a judoka might encounter. The thumb is a more intricate joint and requires more care. Jammed thumbs are not only uncomfortable but also make it difficult to grab the opponent with any confidence. While wrapping is a fairly good means of stabilizing the thumb joint and preventing further injury, it will still feel a little restrictive when trying to get a grip tight.

3. **Wrists:** There are 10 bones in the wrist minus the metacarpals, which are supported by muscles and ligaments. Injuries to this area are usually to the bones, ligaments, tendons and/or muscles. So no matter what, strapping or taping this area can aid in supporting and stabilizing the entire joint.

4. **Elbows:** Injuries to the elbow occur for various reasons, like when you place your arm down incorrectly during a fall or when your opponent executes an overly exuberant armbar application on you. When correctly strapped, the arm should not be able to fully extend, much less hyperextend.

5. **Ankles:** What maintains the proper range of motion for this joint is the shape of the articulating bones, the attaching ligaments, tendons and muscles. Sprains and strains are usually caused when a piece of this area is stretched or torn.

6. **Toes:** While toes aren't bent to the same degree as fingers, the nature of our toes is to bear the weight of the body. Thus, the area of the toes widens when the foot is planted on the ground. This happens often in judo so it should be no surprise that toes get sprained. The usual method of supporting a toe, as with fingers, is to tape the injured toe to the adjoining toe for support.

Before taping an injury ask when and how the injury occurred. Try to determine the extent of the injury before taking any action. Is the area swollen, inflamed, discolored, open or deformed in any way? Next, gently palpate the area and ask the competitor if anything hurts. Determine the angle at which the injury seems to cause pain. If the pain is excruciating, it is usually advisable to transport the individual to a medical facility. Should there be excessive pain or discomfort, it is always best to consult with a medical professional. For a more in-depth look at methods of wrapping and strapping, there are courses available at most kinesiology programs at four-year institutions.

Wrapping/Strapping Fingers

1: Using one-and-a-half-inch tape, begin with the first digit.

2: To support the injured finger, it is best to tape it to the adjacent finger, in a bent position and slightly apart if you are planning to practice. This will allow for the expansion of both fingers as they bend so you can still maintain a proper grip in practice or competition.

3: Place a second strip on the next knuckle and in the same manner, allowing expansion when the fingers are bent.

4: Have the athlete flex his fingers to see how he feels.

Wrapping/Strapping Thumbs

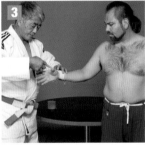

1-2: First an anchor strip is applied to the wrist area in order to anchor the strips that will wrap around the thumb. It is probably not necessary to apply pre-wrap here.

3-4: Next, apply your first strip of tape, which should be long enough to circumvent the thumb and crisscross but still anchor the strip to the wrist anchor strip.

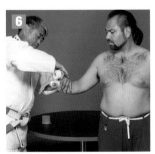

5: Three or four of these strips should be applied to completely cover the thumb joint.

6: Now, place your last strip over the anchor and ends of the over-lapping strips to lock your tape job in place.

Wrapping/Strapping Wrists

1: Have the athlete flex or extend his hurt wrist. Whatever direction causes further pain is the direction you want to restrict movement in. Strapping will prevent the wrist from going in that direction. Here, the athlete's pain is enhanced when he moves his wrist in a downward direction.

2: After the pre-wrap is in place, apply anchor strips to both the hand and the wrist. If upward movement of the hand causes pain, have the athlete bend his wrist downward because the taping job should be done such that moving in that direction doesn't cause pain.

3: Next, apply bridging strips that go from the hand to the wrist anchor, one straight and two crisscrossed.

4: Now apply your lock strips over the anchor strips. The more you want to restrict movement in one direction, the more bend or gap you should have on the opposite side as you create your bridge. As you place your lock strips it is best not to continually wind the tape around the wrist, but rather cut individual strips to lock in place. Continual wrapping usually ends up cutting off circulation as each revolution draws it tighter.

Wrapping/Strapping Elbows

1: First, apply the pre-wrap to the area to which the anchor strips will be applied.

2: Wrap the pre-wrapped area to prepare your anchor points.

3: With the elbow flexed, place three or four bridging strips across from one anchor point to the other.

4: Bending or straightening before placing the bridging strips will determine how much range of motion the athlete will have. The more flexion, the less range of motion allowed.

 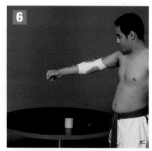

5: Finally, place the lock strips over the bridge and anchor strips.

6: Have the athlete extend the arm and test the taping job. Ask the athlete how the job feels. Is it too tight or too loose?

Wrapping/Strapping Ankles

1: When injured, first pre-wrap the area, then place an anchor strip about one third of the way up the lower leg.

2-3: Depending on where the injury has occurred, you will start the stirrup from the opposite side of the injury at the anchor strip and run the tape down the foot, around the bottom of the foot, and up to the anchor strip on the opposite side. Keep the tape flat against the surface to avoid creases and air pockets.

4: Next, lock the ankle in place with a figure-8 pattern that begins by placing the tape on the instep and goes around the foot.

5-6: Follow the contour of the foot and proceed around the area above the ankle, around the lower leg and down the side of the foot. Go under and around again, thus making a figure-8 pattern. As this is done, try to cover areas previously not covered before or else the exposed skin could develop blisters or skin irritations. This can be repeated two or three times.

7: Should there be any areas not covered between the anchor strips and instep, cover them to avoid possible blistering.

8: Have the athlete stand and test the taping job. If it is too tight, you may have to start over again. The more you do these taping jobs the better feel you will get for what is needed. Remember to ask your athlete questions.

Wrapping/Strapping Toes

1: Using one-and-a-half-inch tape, begin taping between the injured digit and the supporting one. Make certain that your strips are long enough to circle both toes and that they allow the athlete to step down without binding the toes together too tightly.

2: The first strip should start near the base of the toe, and the second strip should start at the distal end of the toe. On all your taping and strapping, have the athlete test out the taping job and ask if it feels too loose or too tight. Is the athlete able to function with ease or does the taping hinder more than help him?

Abrasions

Due to the abrasive nature of materials that make up a judogi, especially double weaves, judoka often find that their skin becomes tender around the knuckles, sometimes even to the point of bleeding. To avoid pain, blood stains to the judogi, and the risk of bloodborne diseases, do the following:

1. Clean the injured area with an antiseptic.
2. Dry the area.
3. Place a adhesive bandage over the wounds.
4. Place athletic tape over them.

Be sure to make allowances for the expansion of your fingers when they are bent. The circumference of your finger will increase in size, but the tape may not, which can impede your ability to get a good grip, not to mention make you uncomfortable. Thus, you can avoid all this by placing the bandage on your fingers when they are in a bent position.

Photo by Eric Nishioka

In addition to alleviating discomfort, properly taped fingers protect your hand from further injury during competition.

True/False

1. In the event of an injured finger, splint the athlete up and he will be ready to practice.

2. Taping supports the joint.

3. It is best to wrap tape tightly around the injury to avoid slippage.

4. Pre-wrap is used to enable the tape to hold better.

5. For excessive discomfort or pain, it's best to consult a medical professional.

Answers: 1.f, 2.t, 3.f, 4.t, 5.t

Chapter Review

1. List at least five items that should be on the stellar coach's checklist.

2. List three things that can aid in cutting down on injuries.

3. Explain what half randori is and its possible benefits.

4. Discuss the differences between ballistic and static stretching.

5. What does the acronym RICE stand for?

6. Explain why rest may be the best remedy.

7. How does ice help an injury? Explain.

8. Explain when taping may or may not help an injured athlete.

9. List at least three items needed in wrapping.

10. What are a few caveats that should be noted in taping fingers and toes?

"The measure of a man's character is what he would do if he knew he would never be found out."

—Thomas Macaulay, English writer

Risk Management

CHAPTER ELEVEN
Risk Management

Situation No. 1: Before class, a few judoka are having a piggyback jousting session, wherein two different athletes are mounted on the shoulders of two other individual athletes and try to knock the mounted partner off. This escalates in intensity and difficulty until one mounted judoka falls, suffers a concussion and a broken arm.

Situation No. 2: There are 25 to 30 judo students packed on to a 20-by-20 mat area. Everyone is busy with randori, trying to throw someone else. When a student succeeds, he doesn't just throw his opponent. Instead, he throws his opponent into the leg of a neighboring competitor as well as a few others. Students collide, judoka roll off the mat space and the end results are several bruises, stubbed toes, bent fingers and an ACL operation.

Situation No. 3: It's a particularly hot day, and the dojo has no air conditioning. A student faints while trying to participate in some competition preparation. His skin is clammy, his breathing is shallow and he hasn't come to. So what do you do now?

For coaches especially, situations like those mentioned above can lead to legal problems. Coaches and instructors are entrusted with the care and development of their students and competitors. The old adage, "do unto other as you would have them do unto you," is as good a place to start as any. To avoid legal issues, the coach or instructor should treat his charges with the care he would want himself. However, the truth is that coaches and instructors need to be a cut above the average person on the street. They need to be vigilant to perilous conditions, especially because competitors, athletes and parents of athletes want nothing more than a clean, safe environment for their loved ones to grow up healthy in.

The examples cited above are instances, however, where, due to neglect or lack of understanding, a judoka is needlessly injured. This can open the coach or instructor or even competitor to legal charges. Thus, the area of law this chapter is concerned about is the aspect of negligence that falls under tort law.

Queries

1. What is negligence about?

2. Are there certain standards for coaches that differ from those for regular people?

3. What defense can there be for negligence?

Negligence

Negligence occurs when there is an assumed duty that is breached or not performed, and you are the proximate cause that has resulted in some damage to another person. Thus, negligence is a result of a duty, breach of duty, causation and damages. For example, you are a bus driver who likes to eat while driving. One day, you don't notice that the car in front of you has braked quickly to avoid going through a red light. You crash into the car. Your duty is to safely transport people. You breached that duty by eating. You are the proximate cause of the accident. Any damages to persons or property become your liability.

However, if any one of these factors is missing, then a case for negligence or liability is very weak. So in our example, if you caused the accident when no one was on the bus and/or the crash didn't result in damage to anyone or the car, then a negligence case brought against you would be weak.

Here are some important terms that relate to negligence cases:

1. **Reasonable man rule:** The "reasonable man rule" represents an objective standard by which any individual's conduct can be measured. In the case of coaches and competitors, this rule states that the standard of care that should be exhibited by a person is that which a sane and reasonable man under same and similar conditions would do. Ergo, a coach is not expected to perform first aid at the same level as a doctor or vice versa. Your expected standard of care is that of your training level.

2. **Foreseeability:** This is a concept that asks the question, Could a sane and reasonable person under the same conditions understand what would happen as the result of one's action or inaction? In the examples in the introduction of this chapter, situations were stated that showed judoka getting hurt. Young students may not see a problem with jousting on piggyback, but an instructor or coach who is trying to maintain a safe environment is a different story. The coach or instructor should have been able to "foresee" a possible accident waiting to happen.

3. **Thompson vs. Seattle Public School District:** This was a landmark $6.3 million case delineating the duties of a coach. Basically, coaches have a duty to properly instruct, which means they should have a set, written curriculum with set objectives and methods of delivery. Additionally, there is a duty to warn against contraindicated or questionable practices that may be detrimental to the student, like not encouraging students to hydrate well during vigorous bouts of exercise. Lastly, there is a duty to supervise. This duty is even more important if the students are young or the activity is inherently risky. An example of supervision would be how scuba diving has an age requirement as well as a standard ratio of supervisors-to-students in play.

True/False

1. Negligence has to do with a type of law called tort law.

2. In order to have a case for negligence, you only need to prove there is a duty that has been breached and that an individual is the proximate cause.

3. The reasonable man rule assumes that everyone is judged by the common sense of the average man on the street in the same situation.

4. Coaches and instructors are held to a higher standard than the common person on the street.

5. Coaches have a duty to teach and warn students of impending dangers and supervise their activities.

Answers: 1.T, 2.F, 3.F, 4.T, 5.T.

Mitigations and Defenses

There are certain instances when a terrible accident may be excused or mitigated. They include:

1. **Act of God:** This describes an occurrence when a natural disaster is involved, such as lightning, floods, earthquakes, storms, etc. These natural occurrences set a disaster in motion that is the actual cause behind the injury to the student under your supervision.

2. **Not meeting all the requirements of negligence:** Remember the four requirements of negligence: duty, breach of duty, causation and damages. If any of these four elements are missing, then negligence cannot be established. For example, pretend a coach had a duty and breached it. The courts establish that he was the proximate cause; however, no one was injured. The fourth element of damages cannot be established so the coach cannot be held liable.

3. **Assumption of risk:** This is when an individual voluntarily enters into an activity knowing of its inherently dangerous nature. Students entering into skydiving know that there is a possibility

of death should a parachute not open. Gymnasts engage in exercises knowing that one false move may send them flying into a wall or floor, thus resulting in grave injury. Judoka know that there is a possibility of bruises, broken bones and, in unlikely cases, death, because it is a martial art. Most dojo have a waiver and release form that students and parents sign. It is advisable that persons signing in the student verbally explain and ask if the student and/or parent understand what they are signing. This of course still does not excuse a negligent act because if you're negligent, then you're still liable for negligence.

4. *Contributory negligence:* This is when the plaintiff is denied recovery due to his own negligence, even where the defendant may have been negligent as well. Looking back at our example about the bus driver, consider if the car had swerved dangerously in front of the bus. Because the car driver made an unsafe lane change and you, the bus driver, were eating on the job, you both contributed to the problem and are both responsible for the accident.

5. *Comparative negligence:* In comparative negligence, recovery is often based on the percentage of attributable fault. For example, an armbar is applied in practice by two white belts and results in a broken arm. The student with the broken arm claims that there should have been supervision by an instructor. The instructor claims that the white belts were instructed that they were not to practice without the presence of a black belt. While the instructor should have been supervising the practice, the white belts clearly contributed to the accident and should not have been practicing, much less executing, a technique usually reserved for black-belt practitioners.

6. *Government immunity:* At one time, many states did not allow their citizens to sue the state government unless the states had given their consent to do so. Today, many government agencies take out liability insurance, which in effect implies that the claim to government immunity is no longer valid. However, many states still use this doctrine to protect their workers and their budgets. This type of situation may apply to military, police assistance leagues, schools, and parks and recreation departments.

True/False

1. A student loses his balance because of an earthquake. He falls onto another student's leg and breaks it. The student and instructor are liable.

2. Negligence is when there is a duty, breach of duty and damages.

3. Contributory negligence apportions fault on a percentage basis.

4. The taking out of insurance by a government agency may nullify its ability to claim government immunity.

Answers: 1.f, 2.t, 3.f, 4.t.

Suggestions for Risk Management:

- [ ] In addition to a black belt, a coach or instructor should have a teacher certification from a nationally recognized organization or institution.

- [ ] Keep current by attending continuing education classes, coaching clinics and certification classes.

- [ ] Maintain a clean and safe environment for students. Vigilance is key.

- [ ] Maintain close supervision.

- [ ] Have a lesson plan with outcomes to be achieved by certain dates.

- [ ] Keep a dated log of serious incidents that may occur, like disagreements and injuries. You may even want some signed statements as to what occurred for liability purposes.

- [ ] Have a posted procedure list of things to do in the event of an accident. Procedures include where nearby hospitals and police departments are and their phone numbers, where the first aid kit is located, how to notify parents of an emergency: etc.

- [ ] Have a checklist of "do's and don'ts" for students in the dojo. This should be handed to them after chalk talk, one-on-one communication or before they start lessons with you. Ask if they understand what you've just read them.

- [ ] When registering a student into your club or when attending special events like competitions, have the students and/or parents fill out, sign and date all waivers. It is important that they read and understand what they are signing.

- [ ] Be mindful of your professional relationship with your clientele.

Chapter Review

1. Briefly discuss the elements necessary to establish negligence.
2. Discuss at least four of the possible excuses for negligence.
3. List at least six suggestions to manage risk in the dojo.

LIST OF REFERENCES BY CHAPTER

CHAPTER 1

Bates, L. A. *Your Ten- to Fourteen-Year-Old.* New York, NY: Dell Publishing, 1989

Brousse, Michel and David Matsumoto. *Judo: A Sport and a Way Of Life.* Seoul, Korea: Ippon Books, 1999

De Mars, AnnMaria. California State/Nanka Coaching Conference. Los Angeles City College, Los Angeles, CA 2008

Ferguson, Howard E. *The Edge: The Guide to Fulfilling Dreams, Maximizing Success and Enjoying a Lifetime of Achievement.* Cleveland, OH: The Edge Company, 1990

Nishioka, Hayward. *Assistant Instructors Certification Manual.* San Francisco, CA: Palacio Publications, 2007

Randall, Wilbur. Coaching Conference at the Olympic Training Center. Colorado Springs, CO 2007

Seidler, Burton. Lecture. California State University at Los Angeles, CA 1971

CHAPTER 2

Angus, Ron. *Competitive Judo.* Champaign, IL: Human Kinetics, 2005

Ferguson, Howard E. *The Edge: The Guide to Fulfilling Dreams, Maximizing Success and Enjoying a Lifetime of Achievement.* Cleveland, OH: The Edge Company, 1990

LeBell, Gene and L.C. Coughran. *The Handbook of Judo.* New York, NY: Cornerstone Library 1962

Nishioka, Hayward. *Assistant Instructors Certification Manual.* San Francisco, CA: Palacio Publications, 2009

Palacio, Mitchell. Lecture on "Periodization." City College of San Francisco, CA 2009

CHAPTER 3

Brousse, Michel and David Matsumoto. *Judo in the U.S.: A Century of Dedication.* Berkeley, CA: North Atlantic Books, 2005

Gleeson, Geof. *Judo Inside Out.* New York, NY: Sterling Publishing Company, 1983

Nishioka, Hayward. *Assistant Instructors Certification Manual.* San Francisco, CA: Palacio Publications, 2009

IJF Refereeing Commission. "The International Judo Federation Competition Rules." www.internationaljudofederation.com, 2009

Power Judo 3: Get a Grip. Hayward Nishioka. A United States Judo Federation Video Production, 2000

Advanced Judo Tactics. Nishioka, Hayward. A Westhill Enterprises Video Production

CHAPTER 4

Alexey, Leitsky, Vladimir Putin and Shestakov, Vasily. *Judo History, Theory, Practice.* Berkeley, CA: Blue Snake Books, 2004

Cousens, Sarah and Yasuhiro Yamashita. *The Fighting Spirit of Judo (Special Interest).* London, UK: Ippon Books Limited, 1993

Kashiwazaki, Katsuhiko. *Fighting Judo.* New York, NY: Viking Press, 1984

Kudo, Kazuzo. *Dynamic Judo.* Tokyo, Japan: Japan Publications Trading Company, 1967

Mifune, Kyuzo. *Canon of Judo: Principle and Technique.* Tokyo, Japan: Seibundo-Shinkosha, 1960

Ohlenkamp, Neil. *Judo Unleashed: Essential Throwing & Grappling Techniques for Intermediate to Advanced Martial Artists.* Boston, MA: McGraw Hill, 2006

Sharp, Harold, E. and Shinzo Takagaki. *Techniques of Judo.* Tokyo, Japan: Tuttle Publishing, 1956

Yeoh, Oon Oon. *Great Judo Championships of the World.* London, UK: Ippon Books Limited, 1993

CHAPTER 5

Ferguson, Howard E. *The Edge: The Guide to Fulfilling Dreams, Maximizing Success and Enjoying a Lifetime of Achievement.* Cleveland, OH: The Edge Company, 1990

Sharp, Harold E. Lecture on "Video Scouting." Los Angeles City College, CA 2009

Tzu, Sun. *The Art of War.* New York, NY: Oxford University Press, 1963

CHAPTER 6

Bradley, Bill. *Values of the Game.* New York, NY: Broadway Books, 2000

Ferguson, Howard E. *The Edge: The Guide to Fulfilling Dreams, Maximizing Success and Enjoying a Lifetime of Achievement.* Cleveland, OH: The Edge Company, 1990

Maslow, Abraham. "A Theory of Human Motivation." *Psychological Review* 50(4) 1943 370-96

Osako, Johnny. Lecture on "Critiquing Referees On the Occasion of the 1979 Desert Classics Judo Championships." AZ 1979

Oka, Dan. Lecture on "Pep Talking and Performance." The National AAU Judo Championships. CA 1959

Seidler, Burton, Ph.D. Lecture on "Motivation and Coaching." California State University at Los Angeles, CA 1973

Skinner, B.F. *The behavior of organisms: An experimental analysis, (The Century psychology series).* New York, NY: D. Appleton & Company, 1938

CHAPTER 7

Brousse, Michel and David Matsumoto. *Judo in the U.S.: A Century of Dedication.* Berkeley, CA: North Atlantic Books, 2005

Cleland, John M.D. Lecture. World Police and Fire Games in Vancouver, Canada 2009

Draeger, Donn and Isao Inokuma. *Weight Training for Championship Judo.* Tokyo, Japan: Kodansha LTD, 1966

Ferguson, Howard E. *The Edge: The Guide to Fulfilling Dreams, Maximizing Success and Enjoying a Lifetime of Achievement.* Cleveland, OH: The Edge Company, 1990

Fisher, A. Garth and Clayne R. Jensen. *Scientific Basis of Athletic Conditioning.* Philadelphia, PA: Lea & Febiger, 1990

Matsumoto, David. United States Judo Federation Conference. San Francisco State University, CA 2000

Palacio, Mitchell. Lecture at City College of San Francisco, CA 2008

Tara Parker-Pope, "Recalibrated Formula Eases Women's Workout," *New York Times,* July 5, 2010 (http://well.blogs.nytimes.com/2010/07/05/recalibrated-formula-eases-womens-workouts/)

CHAPTER 8

Draeger, Donn and Isao Inokuma. *Weight Training for Championship Judo.* Tokyo, Japan: Kodansha Ltd, 1966

Fleck, Steven J. and William J. Kraemer. *Designing Resistance Training Programs.* Champaign, IL: Human Kinetics Publishers, 1987

Ferguson, Howard E. *The Edge: The Guide to Fulfilling Dreams, Maximizing Success and Enjoying a Lifetime of Achievement.* Cleveland, OH: The Edge Company, 1990

Flores, Dr. Jacob. Lecture on "Fast, Slow, and Intermediate Muscle Fibers." 2009

Hay, James G. and Gavin J. Reid. *Anatomy, Mechanics, and Human Motion.* Englewood Cliffs, NJ: Prentice Hall, 1988

Stone, Michael H. Olympic Training Center Coaching Conference. CO 1997

CHAPTER 9

Hales, Diane. *An Invitation to Health.* Florence, KY: Brooks Cole, 2008

Pollan, Michael. *In Defense of Food.* New York, NY: Penguin Books, 2008

Shils, M. et al, *Modern Nutrition in Health and Disease,* Lea and Febiger, Philadelphia, PA 1994

Wildman, Robert and Barry Miller. *Sports and Fitness Nutrition (with Info Track).* Florence, KY: Brooks Cole, 2004

Williams, Melvin H. *Nutrition for Health, Fitness and Sport.* Boston, MA: McGraw-Hill, 2002

CHAPTER 10

Arnheim, Daniel D. and Carl E. Klafs. *Modern Principles of Athletic Training.* Saint Louis, MO: The C. V. Mosby Company, 1969

Cleland, John M.D. Lecture on "Injuries in Competitive Judo." World Police and Fire Games in Vancouver, Canada 2009

Ferguson, Howard E. *The Edge: The Guide to Fulfilling Dreams, Maximizing Success and Enjoying a Lifetime of Achievement.* Cleveland, OH: The Edge Company, 1990

Roy, Steven. *Sport's Medicine Prevention, Evaluation, Management & Rehabilitation.* Englewood Cliff, NJ: Prentice Hall, 1983

CHAPTER 11

Adam, S. and Bayless, M. "How the Seattle decision affects liability and you." *Facility Planning for Health, Physical Activity, Recreation and Sport: Concepts and Applications,* edited by Thomas H. Sawyer. Urbana IL: Sagamore Publishing, 2002

ABOUT THE AUTHOR

Hayward Nishioka was born in Los Angeles to a migrant household in a hostile post-World War II America. When he was 12 years old, his mother remarried Dan Oka, who changed the course of Nishioka's life. Oka was a second-degree black belt in judo at the time, and he became Nishioka's first instructor. In 1965, Nishioka joined Sen Shin *dojo,* which was headed by Ryusei Inouye. By the time Nishioka was 17 years old, he had earned his black belt and won third place in the National AAU Judo Championships.

Since then, Nishioka has participated and won multiple national and international judo competitions. He received the gold medal at the 1967 International Pan American Games. He also has been a part of World Judo Championship teams, representing the United States in 1965 and 1967 as a team member and representing the country in 1987, 1993, 1995, 1997 and 1999 as assistant coach of video scouting. Nishioka also served as head coach for the Pan American championships and World University Games, as well as several other international events. In 1984, he was a training site manager for the Los Angeles Olympics. In 1996, he was an international "A" level referee for the Olympics in Atlanta.

Nishioka is currently a full professor of kinesiology at Los Angeles City College. He also instructs judo.

COMPETITIVE PROFILE	EVALUATOR: _____	EVENT: _____

DATE: _____/_____/_____

VERSUS

NAME: _____ REP: _____	NAME: _____ REP: _____
DIVISION: _____ ROUND: _____	DIVISION: _____ ROUND: _____

STANCE:
- ☐ Right
- ☐ Left
- ☐ Middle

GRIPS:

Comments: _____
_____
_____
_____
_____

STANCE:
- ☐ Right
- ☐ Left
- ☐ Middle

GRIPS:

Comments: _____
_____
_____
_____
_____

TECHNIQUES: Right   Left
1. _____   _____
2. _____   _____
3. _____   _____
4. _____   _____
5. _____   _____

GRIP TO TIME OF ATTACK: ☐ Fast   ☐ Medium   ☐ Slow

Comments: _____
_____
_____
_____
_____

TECHNIQUES: Right   Left
1. _____   _____
2. _____   _____
3. _____   _____
4. _____   _____
5. _____   _____

GRIP TO TIME OF ATTACK: ☐ Fast   ☐ Medium   ☐ Slow

Comments: _____
_____
_____
_____
_____

ATTACKS PER MINUTE (APM):   Throw

```
   1  2  3  4  5
1. ☐  ☐  ☐  ☐  ☐    Y  W  W  I  _____
2. ☐  ☐  ☐  ☐  ☐    Y  W  W  I  _____
3. ☐  ☐  ☐  ☐  ☐    Y  W  W  I  _____
4. ☐  ☐  ☐  ☐  ☐    Y  W  W  I  _____
5. ☐  ☐  ☐  ☐  ☐    Y  W  W  I  _____
```

ATTACKS PER MINUTE (APM):   Throw

```
   1  2  3  4  5
1. ☐  ☐  ☐  ☐  ☐    Y  W  W  I  _____
2. ☐  ☐  ☐  ☐  ☐    Y  W  W  I  _____
3. ☐  ☐  ☐  ☐  ☐    Y  W  W  I  _____
4. ☐  ☐  ☐  ☐  ☐    Y  W  W  I  _____
5. ☐  ☐  ☐  ☐  ☐    Y  W  W  I  _____
```

PENALTIES: (Minutes) ☐ 1   ☐ 2   ☐ 3   ☐ 4   ☐ 5
F/A, NC, 5 Seconds, One Side, Outside, Etc.:
Comments: _____
_____
_____

PENALTIES: (Minutes) ☐ 1   ☐ 2   ☐ 3   ☐ 4   ☐ 5
F/A, NC, 5 Seconds, One Side, Outside, Etc.:
Comments: _____
_____
_____

WIN/LOSS BY: _____ **TOTAL TIME:** _____

WIN/LOSS BY: _____ **TOTAL TIME:** _____

GRIPS: BREAKS, MAKE, CONTROL, CHANGES

Comments: _____

_____

_____

_____

_____

TRANSITIONS STANDING TO MAT:

MAT: Offense: ☐ 1   ☐ 2   ☐ 3   ☐ 4"   ☐ 5

       Defense: ☐ 1   ☐ 2   ☐ 3   ☐ 4   ☐ 5

Techniques:

TACTICS:

OBSERVED WEAKNESSES:
Past, Present, Condition, Strength, Technical, Mat, Etc.:

PLAN OF ATTACK:

GRIPS: BREAKS, MAKE, CONTROL, CHANGES

Comments: _____

_____

_____

_____

_____

TRANSITIONS STANDING TO MAT:

MAT: Offense: ☐ 1   ☐ 2   ☐ 3   ☐ 4   ☐ 5

       Defense: ☐ 1   ☐ 2   ☐ 3   ☐ 4   ☐ 5

Techniques:

TACTICS:

OBSERVED WEAKNESSES:
Past, Present, Condition, Strength, Technical, Mat, Etc.:

PLAN OF ATTACK:

FORM DESIGN BY: HAYWARD NISHIOKA

ENJOY THESE OTHER GREAT BOOKS
FROM BLACK BELT

To order, call toll-free: (800) 581-5222 or visit www.blackbeltmag.com/shop